Vegetarian
nosh 4 students

17

a fun cookbook
for
students

Joy May

©2006 Joy May

Published by:
inTRADE (GB) Ltd, 25 Greenway, Letchworth Garden City, Herts, SG6 3UG, UK
Contact: joymay@mac.com

Author: Joy May

ISBN: 0-9543179-4-7

1st Printed June 2006

Printed in Thailand

Introduction

This recipe book is a sequel to nosh4students, which I wrote when my eldest son, Benjamin, left for university. Since then I have seen a need to produce a book just for vegetarians. Being a vegetarian often means buying 'fast food' can be problematic. Cooking, therefore becomes a necessary skill. The layout of this book aims to make cooking easy and inspiring: there is a photo of each recipe that ought to help.

The stars ✱ ✱ ✱ ✱ ✱ are an indication of how difficult the recipes are. A one-star recipe is very quick and easy; five stars are for you to try when you are a little more accomplished or have a bit more time. Most of the food in this book is healthy and well balanced, though there is the odd, over-indulgent one!

The original nosh4students has about 60 vegetarian or vegetarian-alternative recipes, so if you like this book it may be worth your purchasing the original one.

The recipes are planned so that you need to use the minimum of pans, dishes and utensils. You need use NO WEIGHING SCALES. A list of cooking equipment to take with you to University is on the next page. I have included a hand held liquidiser on the list, you can buy one for about five Pounds and it will help you to make soups, sauces and smoothies.

Dedicated to Tim.

Author
Joy May

Contents

Limited Utensils

These recipes have been written
so that you will be able to produce them
using just the following utensils:

To measure:
mug (approx. ½ pint)
tablespoon (the size mum serves with)
dessertspoon (the one you eat cereal with)
teaspoon

To prepare and cook with:
wooden spoon
chopping board
sharp knife
small pan with lid
medium sized pan with lid
slotted turner (fish slice)
frying pan
casserole dish with lid
colander
flat roasting dish or metal non-stick cooking tray
microwaveable plate
cheese grater
hand-held blender
loaf tin
mixing bowl
jug.

What do I do If ??????

Everything I cook in the oven is burnt or undercooked - If you have an older oven, it could b
that the thermostat is not working quite as well as it should. Don't give up; just adjust it
lowering or lifting the temperature you normally set it to.

All the oven temperatures in the book are based on degrees centigrade, in a fan oven. He
is a chart to help you adjust the temperature if this is not the case in your kitchen.

Gas Mark	°C	Fan °C	°F	Oven Temperature
¼	110	90	225	Very cool
½	120	100	250	Very cool
1	140	120	275	Cool
2	150	130	300	Cool
3	160	140	325	Warm
4	180	160	350	Moderate
5	190	170	375	Moderately hot
6	200	180	400	Fairly hot
7	220	200	425	Hot
8	230	210	450	Very hot
9	240	220	475	Very hot

How long can I keep this before it kills me

Eggs - 2 to 3 weeks
Milk - 2 days once opened. Unopened it should keep until the 'best before' date, b
must remain in the fridge.
Butter and margarine spreads - 2 to 3 weeks
Cheese - I week once opened, 2 weeks unopened. Keep cheese wrapped with cling filr
or it will go dry and horrid. Green mould on cheese, other than the blue varieties, mear
that it is best thrown away.
Vegetables - These vary. Some keep better in the fridge, others don't. Onions ar
potatoes - Keep for about one week; out of the fridge and in a dark place. Onc
potatoes have gone green, they are not very good for you!
Green vegetables - These keep better in the fridge, as do carrots, parsnips, etc.
Salad, lettuce, cucumber, tomatoes, peppers, etc. - Keep in the fridge for up to a week.
Keep lettuce covered.

Keep everything covered in the fridge. This helps things keep better and rules o
cross-contamination if you share a fridge with carnivores, or someone who leave
disgusting things in there! Cling film is a wonderful and inexpensive invention.

Don't keep tins in the fridge. Once opened, the tin will begin to make the food taste of
metal, and won't do you much good.

What does this mean ?

If you are used to cooking, this page may seem a little elementary. However, if you are a fresher and have been used to mum doing the cooking, some of these explanations may be helpful.

Coring an apple - Generally, you can quarter the apple to remove the core. But if you are making baked apples; get a sharp knife, put the apple on a cutting board, and with a downward and circular movement cut out the core without breaking up the apple. Don't do this towards your hand unless you want to visit A & E.

Folding - Do this with a metal spoon. Slowly and gently sweep the spoon across the bottom of the bowl and draw it towards yourself, then go around the edge of the bowl. Repeat until the mixture is even. It does not mean beat, which is to vigorously mix with a wooden spoon.

Making breadcrumbs - Similar to rubbing in. this works best if the bread is not too fresh. Tear the bread into pieces and then rub it between your fingertips and thumbs. It usually doesn't matter if you cannot get the crumbs too fine.

Oil - I refer to this in many recipes, you can use either vegetable oil, sunflower oil or olive oil.

Root vegetables - I make reference to these in a few of the recipes. They are simply vegetables that grow under the ground. The most common ones are potatoes, carrots, swedes, turnips, parsnips, sweet potatoes, and celeriac.

Rubbing in butter - There are a few crumble and biscuit recipes where I have asked you to 'rub in' the butter. All this means is that you gently pick up the flour and butter, and roll it between your thumbs and fingertips. Do this a few times until the butter gets smaller and smaller - very soon it will look like breadcrumbs.

Soaking beans - If you buy dried beans, which are cheaper, you will need to soak them. Some need to be soaked overnight, such as black-eyed beans; others, like yellow split peas, only need to be soaked for an hour. All you need to do is soak them in cold water. Just use a cereal bowl and soak only as many as you need. Always be careful to rinse all beans thoroughly. Even if you are using tinned beans you still need to rinse them well to be on the safe side.

Thicken up with cornflour - Sometimes, as with a stir fry, the liquid may be a bit runny. Simply put a teaspoon of cornflour in a mug and mix with a tablespoon of water until it is smooth. Add to the pan and stir well. The liquid should thicken.

Toast nuts - Simply pre-heat the grill, place the nuts on the baking tray, and put it under the grill. Watch them carefully, as they brown very quickly.

Turn out into a tray - Using the baking tray, evenly pour or spoon stuff onto it.

Whizz - I have recommended that you buy a hand-held blender. When I refer to 'whizz', I simply mean blend.

Basics

Balanced diet

You will know, as a vegetarian, that is important for you to think carefully about the food you eat if you are to stay healthy. Just to eat loads of pasta or even just loads of vegetables, is not really sufficient. There are many good sources of proteins, vitamins, and minerals to be found. Below are some general guidelines to eating healthily as a vegetarian. There are many sites on the internet if you require more detailed information.

Daily intake

3-4 •portions of cereals, grains, or potatoes   •one portion = one serving
4-5 portions of fruit, or vegetables
2-3 portions of pulses, nuts, or seeds
2 portions of milk, cheese, eggs, or soya
a small quantity of vegetable oil, butter, or margarine

Carbohydrates
This is our main energy source, though too much carbohydrate is not good for you. Sources include: bread, white rice, potatoes and other root vegetables, pasta, sweets, and chocolate.

Proteins
These are 'body builders' ; not just to develop muscle, but to keep our cartilage, hair, skin, and blood in good shape. Sources include: dairy products, grains, cereals, pulses, seeds, nuts, and eggs.

Fats
We do need some fat in our diet, but it is essential not to overdo it. Try to eat fats which are high in monounsaturated and polyunsaturated fats. Cheese contains approximately one third fat. The temptation for some vegetarians is to eat lots of cheese, and this is not generally a good idea. Sources include: cheeses, margarines and butters, pastries, crisps, chips, eggs, and chocolate.

Vitamins and Minerals.
If you eat a balanced diet, you will get the vitamins and minerals you need. Milk is an excellent balanced source of protein, carbohydrate, and fat. Of course if you drink low-fat milk, it is much better for you. Milk also contains lots of minerals and vitamins; it is an excellent source of calcium. The one thing it does lack is iron. Vegetarians need to make sure they get enough iron in order to keep their blood count healthy.

Spirulina
Spirulina is known as a 'superfood'. It is a microscopic algae and contains the highest concentration of nutrients found in any one food, plant, grain, or herb. Weight for weight it contains twelve times as much digestible protein as beef. It is known to significantly increase energy and stamina levels as well as boost the immune system. It is an excellent food supplement for vegetarians. If you need more information and good pricing on this please email me at joymay@mac.com

Specific sources of good nutrition

Soya and mycoproteins

Soya is very important to vegetarians as it is the only vegetable protein to contain amino acids. Soya beans are low in cholesterol and unsaturated fats and high in calcium. If you do not like products such as tofu you can always drink soya milk. **Sources** - Quorn, soya milk, soya sauce, textured vegetable protein (TVP), and tofu. Tofu is readily available at most supermarkets, either soft, smoked, or marinated. Tofu is also rich in protein and contains calcium, iron, and vitamins B1, B2, and B3.

Fruit and vegetables

Fruit and vegetables are full of fibre and a whole range of vitamins and minerals. They make up an important part of the vegetarian diet. Root vegetables such as potatoes, carrots, swedes, parsnips, etc. are not good to eat in excess. The daily intake guide suggests 4-5 portions of fruit per day. One portion means one piece of fruit or one serving of vegetables; one tablespoon of dried fruit (it is a good idea to have some dried fruit around to eat instead of sweets and chocolate); one glass of fruit juice (a smoothie could equal 2 portions if you put 2 fruits in it); a side salad, or vegetables within a dish, e.g. in a curry.

Pulses, beans, and lentils

These are an important source of protein and iron. Sources include: soya beans, lentils, kidney beans, chickpeas, bortolli beans, black-eyed beans, pinto beans, and haricot beans. Baked beans are very convenient.

Cereals

It is best to use unrefined cereals. They provide proteins, carbohydrates, B vitamins, iron, vitamin E, and some minerals. Sources include: buckwheat (easiest used as flour), corn, oats, rice in its different varieties, wheat, and rye.

Nuts and seeds

A good source of protein, high in essential amino acids, minerals; and a good energy food. They taste better than soya products and are easier to handle in cooking. Keep a small bowl of good nuts around your room and eat instead of sweets and chocolate. **Sources include:** Almond, brazil, cashew, coconut, hazelnut, macadamia, peanuts, pecan, pine nuts, pistachio, walnut, pumpkin seeds, sesame seeds, and sunflower seeds.

Conclusions

Think about what you are going to eat - if possible write a menu for the week. There are some suggested menus on pages 130-133. Planning meals means you waste less food and that you get a good balance of nutrition, as well as saving time on trips to the shops. If, on any one day, you choose to make a dish that has only vegetables, make sure that you eat some nuts and/or cheese. On the next day you may eat a meal with either nuts or soya. There are many recipes in nosh4students where you can exchange the mince for quorn, or the sausages for vegetarian sausages. Have fresh and dried fruit and nuts to hand and get into the habit of eating them. If, by the end of the week, you have fruit that needs eating, make a smoothie! There are very few repeated recipes in this vegetarian nosh4students book, so if you find this book helpful then do buy the other one.

Good buying ideas

1. Look through the recipe book before you go to the supermarket and buy ingredients for specific recipes, this way you will not waste food or be frustrated that you don't have all the ingredients to complete a recipe. See pages 130-133 for sample menus and shopping lists.

2. Look at pages 8 & 9. Make sure that you are getting a balanced diet; decide before you go to the shops what kind of vegetables and fruits you need to buy.

3. Keep things in stock like pasta, rice, flour, cornflour, salt and pepper, tofu, pulses, and tins of beans (not just baked beans). Sun dried tomatoes and pesto are useful in many pasta dishes.

4. Basic things to liven up boring food are: HP sauce, soy sauce, a few freeze-dried herbs (basil, parsley, mixed herbs), stock cubes, pilau rice cubes or pilau rice seasoning, tomato sauce, tomato puree, garlic. Curry paste is much better than curry powder, use it in all sorts of things; liven up baked beans and stir fries for instance.

5. Keep a spare loaf of bread and a pint of milk in the freezer. Don't freeze milk in glass bottles, use the plastic bottles or cartons.

6. Always make sure that when you have visited home you return to uni having creamed off any 'excess' from mum's cupboards.

7. You will need to build up a stock of herbs and spices in order to keep your food tasty and varied.

8. It would be helpful to buy a hand held blender, they are available from supermarkets for about a fiver.

9. A pepper mill would also be good as freshly ground pepper really enhances the taste of food.

Golden rules or helpful suggestions

1. Cooking should be FUN! Most vegetarians are used to cooking as there is not a huge range of ready-made vegetarian meals to buy. If you are not an experienced cook start by choosing the simpler recipes; remember, the stars ★ ★ ★ ★ ★ are an indication of how easy they are.

2. Prepare well. Read the recipe through first to get an idea of what you should be doing. Chop vegetables before you begin to cook.

3. Don't have the heat source too high or leave things on the top of the cooker unattended!

4. If you are living with another vegetarian then cook meals for 2 and share. Stir frys etc. do not reheat well, and you will lose many of the vitamins and minerals if you reheat vegetables.

5. Try to keep things tasty, (e.g. don't cook the same stir fry over and over again). Try new recipes.

6. When frying vegetables, especially onions, make sure you take the time to allow them to brown. This caramelises the starches and sugars in the food, and gives them a much better taste.

7. Try to keep things clean in the kitchen, e.g. chopping boards, dish cloths and tea towels. Even though you are not dealing with meat yourself, if others in the kitchen are, then you need to take extra care.

Basic

How to cook pasta

There are many kinds of pasta to choose from in the shops, often made from different ingredients. Most will have instructions on the packets as to how to cook them. Just in case you have lost the packet, here are some general guidelines:

I. **Spaghetti** For one person, depending on appetite, you will need a bunch of spaghetti approximately the diameter of a 50p piece. Boil sufficient water in a pan to cover the spaghetti whilst cooking - approximately half a pan full. Once the water is boiling, lower the spaghetti sticks into the water. Once the submerged part has softened slightly, push the rest in. Take care not to put your fingers in the water. Simmer for 8-10 minutes. Test one piece to see if it is cooked. Pasta should not be cooked until it is soggy and sticky; some people like it 'al dente', which means firm when bitten i.e. still with a little body to it. This is a matter of preference. Drain the water off and add one teaspoon of butter or olive oil. Mixing this in will stop the spaghetti sticking together.

2. **Most other pastas** Again, boil enough water to cover the pasta. Once the water is boiling, add the pasta. One mug of dried pasta is plenty for one person with a very healthy appetite. Simmer for the appropriate time, drain, and add butter or olive oil to prevent the pasta sticking together.

3. **Cooking times**
Tagliatelle, smaller pasta twists, small macaroni - approx. 5 minutes.
Riccioli, Tirali, Fusilli and thicker twists - 8-11 minutes.
Some varieties of pasta, like Penne, may take as long as 15 minutes to cook.

How to cook rice

There are many different types of rice to buy. I would recommend that you use basmati. It is slightly more expensive than long grain or quick cook rice, but has a much better flavour and texture than the cheaper varieties.
Rice for one person = ½ mug rice + 1 mug water. 1 teaspoon of pilau rice flavouring will transform rice from bland to yummy.

Using a pan with a lid, (cover with tin foil if you don't have a lid), bring the water to the boil. Add the flavour-cube or seasoning, and stir until it has dissolved. Add the rice and stir; bring back to the boil. Once boiling, turn the heat down to very low so that the rice simmers gently. Put the lid on the pan and cook for approximately 15 minutes. Do not stir whilst the rice is cooking or you will make it sticky. The rice should be cooked once the water has disappeared, just tip the pan slightly to see if the water has evaporated. Don't keep lifting the lid, as during the last part of the cooking time the rice is steaming, and you need to keep the heat and the steam in the pan. Test the rice after 15 minutes. If the rice is still too crunchy and the water has all gone, then you have boiled it too quickly. Add a little more water, replace the lid, and cook for another 5 minutes. If the rice is cooked before you have finished cooking the rest of the meal, just leave the pan off the heat, with the lid still on, and it will keep warm for some time.

Vegetables

You don't always need to peel veggies. It is a matter of taste! Washing them, however, is always a good idea. Larger things like potatoes and carrots need to be cut into pieces before cooking; broccoli broken into 'small trees', and so on.

Boiled vegetables Most vegetables need to be cooked in just enough water to cover them. Bring the water to the boil. Once boiling, add the vegetables and a little salt, and simmer gently with the lid on the pan. If you keep the source of the heat low, not only will you preserve more of the nutrients in the vegetables, but you will also avoid burnt pans and very mucky cookers where the pans have boiled over.

Here are some approximate cooking times

Swedes and turnips	20-25 minutes.
Potatoes, parsnips, carrots	10-15 minutes.
Cauliflower	10 minutes.
Broccoli, courgettes	5 minutes, boiling gently.
Green beans, snow peas, mange tout	5-10 minutes.
Spinach	1-2 minutes; just enough to make the leaves wilt. You will only need a little water in the bottom of the pan.
Leeks	5-10 minutes.
Cabbage	5-10 minutes. Again, you only need a little water. Drain after cooking, and add some butter and black pepper. Return to the pan and cook for another 2 minutes to dry the cabbage a little.

If you really want the fuss of **mashed potatoes,** it is best to peel them first. Boil them as described above. Once they are cooked through, mash them with a little butter and milk using either a fork or a potato masher.

Jacket Potatoes see page 14-15.

Roast vegetables. Preheat the oven to 180°C/gas mark 6. Cut the vegetables into medium sized, fairly even pieces. Put them on a flat roasting/baking tray and sprinkle them with salt and olive oil. Turn them over with your hands to make sure that the oil is covering all the pieces. Set them back on the tray with flat sides up. If the flat sides are on the tray itself they will tend to stick. Sprinkle with rosemary if you wish. Put in the middle of the oven for 30 minutes. Check to see if any are getting too brown; maybe the ones around the edge. Move, or turn over as necessary. Put back in the oven for another 30 minutes. If you want to roast peppers, rub them with oil, place on a baking tray and cook for 25 minutes.

Things to roast - potatoes (cut into 2 or 3 pieces), butternut squash (cut into 2" chunks), parsnips (cut into 4 lengthways), sweet potatoes (cut into 2 or 3 pieces), onions (cut into 6 wedges), fennel (cut into 4 wedges). If you want to roast tomatoes; cut the skin, rub with a little oil, and add to the tray about 15 minutes before the end of the cooking time.

Roast vegetables are great with things like beanburgers (page 71), and nut roast (pages 59-63).

Jacket Potatoes

1. Use medium or large potatoes. Always slit the skin with a knife before baking, or it may explode in the oven or the microwave.

2. Bake in the oven at 200°C/gas mark 7 for 1 hour. If you are short of time, cook in the microwave on full power for 5 minutes, and then in the oven for 30 minutes. If you are really short of time, you can cook in the microwave for 7-10 minutes on full power. You will only get the crisp jacket if you cook the potato in the oven. Timing depends on how large the potato is.

3. When the potato is cooked, cut it open and add any of the following suggestions, together with a little butter to moisten:

Baked beans
Grated cheese
Spicy chick peas (page 72)
Bean casserole (page 73)
Cottage cheese, on its own or with sweetcorn, tomatoes, peppers, etc.
Guacamole (easiest to buy) and salsa (page88).
Mushroom stroganoff (page 103)
Refried beans, you can buy these in tins, they will be near fajitas and salsa in the supermarket.
Natural Yogurt, pepper, sweetcorn, chilli powder
Natural yogurt, sliced mushrooms, 1 teaspoon tomato puree, 1 teaspoon mild curry paste
Ratatouille (page 97)

Jacket potatoes taste great served with a little salad, lettuce, tomatoes, cucumber, and spring onions.

Variations

Potato baked twice with pesto

Bake the potato. Cut it in half lengthways, scoop out the soft potato with a spoon, place it in a dish, and mash with a fork. Mix in I tablespoon of thick double cream, I teaspoon of green pesto sauce, a squeeze of lemon juice, and one teaspoon of pine nuts. Season with salt and pepper. Put the potato mixture back into the skin and grate some parmesan cheese over the top. Return to the oven for 10 minutes until the cheese has browned.

Mexican

Bake the potato. Whilst it is baking mix together the following ingredients: I small tin of sweetcorn; ¼ red pepper, finely chopped; I" piece of a cucumber, cut into small cubes; about ¼ onion, finely chopped; I teaspoon curry paste; salt and pepper. Once the potato is cooked, split it open, then add some butter and the filling. You may wish to add some natural yogurt.

Spicy mushroom

Bake the potato. When it has 10 minutes left to cook, fry 4 chopped mushrooms, and a chopped onion for 3-4 minutes. Take off the heat and add ¼ teaspoon of curry paste, ½ mug natural yogurt, and a teaspoon of tomato puree. Mix together and season with salt and pepper. When the potato is cooked , split open and put the filling in.

Cheesy chives

Bake the potato. While it is cooking, mix together ½ x 125g packet of soft cheese, 2 dessertspoons fromage frais, I x 2" cube of blue cheese, crumbled; I stick of finely chopped celery, I teaspoon chives, and 2 chopped spring onions. Season with salt and pepper. When the potato is cooked, split open and put the filling in.

You can vary this recipe using different kinds of cheese; strong cheddar, Double Gloucester etc., mixed with the cream cheese and fromage frais. A strong flavoured cheese will work the best.

Tofu and avocado

Bake the potato. When it has 10 minutes left to cook, start to prepare the filling. Scoop out the flesh of one medium avocado, and mix with ½ x 175g pack of tofu, I teaspoon lemon juice, I spring onion (finely chopped), and I chopped tomato. Season with salt and pepper. When the potato is cooked, cut it in half lengthways and scoop out the soft potato, leaving the skin intact. Mix the potato with the avocado mixture. Put back into the potato skin. Serve with salsa (page 88).

Basics

Bread and stuff

As vegetarians, it is important to eat good bread; granary and wholemeal are good breads to look out for. Try not to eat white bread all the time.

Sandwiches - ideas for fillings

~ Honey and banana
~ Scrambled eggs. You can add some cheese to the egg whilst cooking (page 18).
~ Cottage cheese or cream cheese; both are great with jam, honey, or bananas.
~ Cottage cheese with tomatoes or cucumber; remember to season well.
~ Cream cheese with tomato and ham
~ Egg mayonnaise - hard boiled eggs, chopped and mixed with mayo. Season well.

~ Cheese and tomato
~ Fried egg
~ Marmite!
~ Peanut butter and jam or marmalade
~ Peanut butter and honey and/or bananas
~ Cheese and pickle
~ Cheese and jam; raspberry works well.
~ Boiled egg and tomato
~ Boiled egg and cress

Eggie Bread

Break an egg into a mug and beat with a fork. Pour out onto a plate. Dip a thick slice of bread into the egg and let the bread soak up the egg on both sides. Put 2 teaspoons of butter in a frying pan, and heat until the butter starts to bubble. Add the bread and cook gently until both sides are browned. Serve with beans and HP or tomato sauce. You can make this sweet by adding a dessertspoon of sugar to the egg at the beginning.

Cinnamon toast

Toast 2 slices of bread very lightly on both sides under the grill. Butter one side, and sprinkle with a mixture of 1 dessertspoon of sugar and half a teaspoon of cinnamon. Put back under the grill and toast for a further 2 minutes.

Garlic bread

This works best with medium-sized bread sticks. Finely chop 2 garlic cloves, and mix together with about 2 tablespoons of butter. Make diagonal cuts in the bread stick, but not quite all the way through. Push the garlic butter into the cuts in the bread. Don't use loads because it will be very greasy if you do. Wrap the bread stick in foil and bake in the oven for 6-7 minutes (200°C/gas mark 7).

Here are a few ideas to make your 'stuff on toast' a bit tastier!

Beans on toast with egg on top; great with HP sauce. Toast the bread, heat the beans, and then fry or poach the eggs (page 18).

Cheese on toast - first, very lightly toast the bread, since you will return it to the grill later to cook the cheese. Butter the toast. At this stage you can add things to go under the cheese, such as pickle, marmite, or sliced tomatoes. Slice or grate the cheese and place on top. Make sure the cheese covers the edges of the toast; it will protect the corners of the bread from being burned. Use a slotted turner to put the toast back under the grill. Watch the toast because it will cook quite quickly. You could use the cheese sauce recipe from page 20, adding a pinch of paprika to spice it up, and just pour over the toast. It will be runny, so don't grill it!

Scrambled egg, with or without cheese (page 18).

Pitta bread makes a tasty alternative to sandwiches. It is inexpensive, and readily available in the supermarkets. You can often stuff more filling in them than in a sandwich. You can put almost anything in, but here are a few suggestions:

Salad tossed in dressing, with thick slices of fried halloumi (a type of Cypriot cheese).
Poached egg and wilted spinach (page 13)
Roasted peppers and tomatoes (page 13), with riccotta cheese
Sun dried tomatoes, sliced, with sweet chillies (found in jars), and goat's cheese.
Fetta cheese, with lettuce, tomato, cucumber, and mayo
Cottage cheese, iceberg lettuce, tomato, sliced spring onions or onion rings, and cucumber
Roasted courgette, aubergine, and tomato (page 47), with goat's cheese
Mozzarella cheese, tomato, avocado (sliced. and mayo
Salad, tossed in dressing, tomato, red pepper, avocado, grated carrot, and mayo
Roasted aubergine with hummus
(Iceberg lettuce works well with most of the above because it makes a crispy contrast to the pitta bread.)

Toasted sandwiches

If you can pick up a sandwich maker at a car boot sale, or from the loft at home, it can be useful. When using a sandwich maker, put the buttered side of the bread on the outside. If you make toasted sandwiches under the grill, put the buttered side on the inside, like a normal sandwich. You can use all the above fillings in toasted sandwiches, apart from the ones containing lettuce or cucumber.

Eggs

Poach

1. Use a small pan or frying pan. Half fill with water and add a good pinch of salt. Bring to the boil, then turn down until the water is only just moving.
2. Break the egg into a mug or cup. Gently pour into the water. Do not stir or turn the heat up; just let it cook. It will take 2-4 minutes, depending on the size of the egg.
3. Once the egg has gone opaque, gently lift out with a fish slice and let the water drain from it.
4. Try with beans on toast, and tomato or HP sauce.

Scramble

1. Take a small milk pan (preferably non-stick), and add 2 teaspoons of butter. Heat gently until the butter bubbles.
2. Break the egg into the pan, and add salt and pepper. Stir slowly with a wooden spoon, breaking up the egg yolk.
3. When the egg is almost set, take the pan off the heat. The egg will continue to cook for a short time in its own heat. If you cook it too long, it will become rubbery.
4. You can add grated cheese and/or chopped tomatoes half way through the cooking.

Fry

Not the healthiest way to eat eggs; but if you must, here is how to do it. (They make a great supper snack as fried egg butties.)
1. Heat 2 teaspoons of butter in the frying pan until the butter begins to bubble.
2. Break the egg into a mug, and then gently pour into the frying pan.
3. Cook on a medium heat until the egg is set.
4. If you want a hard yolk, turn the egg over halfway through the cooking using a slotted turner.

Boil

1. Fill a small pan ⅔ full with water and bring to the boil.
2. Lower the egg into the pan on a spoon.
3. Simmer briskly for 3 minutes for a very runny egg; 5 minutes and you will still be able to dip your soldiers in the runny yolk; 12 minutes and it will be hard boiled.

Omelettes

A basic omelette for 1 person

1. Put two or three eggs in a mug, and beat well with a fork. Add two tablespoons of water.
2. Switch on the grill to full heat, and leave to warm up.
3. Melt about a dessertspoon of butter in the frying pan. Once it begins to bubble, pour the egg mixture into the pan.
4. As it sets on the bottom of the pan, gently move the set egg with a fish slice, and allow the runny egg to take its place. Do this with two or three sweeping movements; don't stir or you will get scrambled egg. Repeat this process once more.
5. While there is still a little runny egg on the top, add whatever filling you want, top with cheese (not essential), and place the frying pan under the hot grill. Don't push under the grill too far or the handle will burn. Watch carefully; the omelette should rise. Once it is browned on the top, remove from the grill and turn out onto a plate. Serve with salad, garlic bread, or baked potatoes.

Suggested fillings - cheese, tomato, mushrooms, fried onions, chopped spring onions, wilted spinach (page 13), or any combination of these ingredients.

Sweet omelettes - add fruit (strawberries, raspberries, or blackcurrants are the best kind of fruit), sugar, cinnamon, or jam.

Sauces

Some vegetarian dishes tend to be a little dry. Here are a few different sauces that you can use to enhance meals. Try them out and see which ones you like.

Pepper sauce

1½ red peppers
½ onion
1 clove garlic
1 tablespoon cream
½ teaspoon sugar
salt and pepper

Fry the chopped peppers, onions, and garlic in a saucepan over a medium heat for 5-8 minutes until they are really soft. Add the sugar. Use the hand-held blender to liquidise. Add the cream, and season well with salt and freshly ground black pepper. You can add half a teaspoon of chilli powder if you like.

Quick Cheese Sauce

1 mug grated cheese
1 tablespoon flour
1 teaspoon butter
1 mug milk
pinch of paprika
salt and pepper

Mix the cheese, paprika, and flour in a saucepan. Make sure that the flour is evenly distributed. Add the milk and stir well. Add the butter. Bring to the boil, and stir frequently - especially as the sauce begins to boil. It should thicken. Season with salt and pepper. This sauce is used in many recipes.

Tomato Sauce

1 onion, chopped
1 clove garlic
2 teaspoons tomato puree
1 teaspoon sugar
salt and pepper
1 teaspoon herbs
1 vegetable stock cube
¼ mug water
oil to fry

Fry the onions and garlic in oil in a saucepan for 4-5 minutes. Add the rest of the ingredients and bring to the boil. Break up the stock cube before you put it in. Turn down to simmer for 10 minutes. Whizz with the blender. You can add HP sauce or chilli sauce if you wish.

Sauces

Peanut sauce

2 tablespoons crunchy peanut butter
1 dessertspoon soy sauce
2 tablespoons coconut milk
1 teaspoon tomato puree
1 teaspoon sugar

Mix everything together and you are ready to go!

Pouring tomato sauce

1 small onion, chopped finely
1 clove garlic, chopped
oil to fry
1 x 400g tin chopped tomatoes
1 teaspoon sugar
1 vegetable stock cube
1 teaspoon mixed herbs
salt and pepper

Fry the onions and garlic in a saucepan for 3-4 minutes, allowing them to brown a little. Add the rest of the ingredients, bring to the boil and allow to simmer for 5 minutes. You can add HP sauce to make a barbecue sauce.

Sweet and sour sauce

2 tablespoons tomato puree
3 tablespoons sugar
2 tablespoons white wine vinegar
1 tablespoon soy sauce
2 teaspoons cornflour
1 mug water

Mix the cornflour and the water in a saucepan until smooth.
Add the rest of the ingredients and bring to the boil.

Basics

Smoothies ★

Serves 1-2 people   Preparation time: 2 mins

Smoothies are an excellent and pleasant way of consuming very healthy foodstuffs. For a balanced and healthy breakfast try the banana, honey and yogurt smoothie. There are loads of smoothies on sale in the supermarkets, but this is a way of producing your own for a fraction of the cost. Do it yourself also means that you have fresh fruits, and therefore maximise the intake of vitamins, etc. You will need a hand-held blender and a jug to blend the fruits in.

Banana, honey, and yogurt. Break up the banana a little, add 2 tablespoons yogurt, 1 dessertspoon honey, and enough apple juice or milk to thin. Whizz.

Strawberries. A handful of strawberries, 1 tablespoon of strawberry yogurt, a few drops of vanilla extract, and a little apple juice or milk. Whizz.

Keep a pack of frozen fruits of the forest in your freezer. Use about 2 tablespoons with 1 tablespoon of yogurt. Add orange juice, or apple juice to make the smoothie thin enough to drink.

Mango. Peel and cut up the mango. Add 2 tablespoons yogurt, a pinch of cinnamon, and mineral water to thin down the smoothie to drinking consistency. Whizz.

Strawberries, raspberries, blackberries. Add about a handful of one type of any of these fruits. Whizz, and add apple juice to thin to a drinking consistency.

Oranges. Finely grate a little of the orange rind. Peel the orange, discard the peel. Add a peeled, chopped apple and some apple juice. Whizz together.

If you have any coconut milk left over from a recipe, mix it together with a banana, apple, or any other fruit you may have around.

Apple, banana, and yogurt. Peel and slice the fruit. Add the yogurt and a little milk. Whizz.

Melon, strawberries, and yogurt. Use about one quarter of a melon, 6-7 strawberries, and 1 tablespoon yogurt. Cut them all up, add together, and whizz.

Spirulina. If you have not heard of this it is an excellent food supplement for vegetarians. See page 8 for more information. Spirulina contains loads of protein and natural minerals. To make the smoothies: 3 tablets, crushed, 3 tablespoons natural yogurt, one banana, peeled and broken up, and 1 dessertspoon honey. Whizz.

Carrot, apple, and celery. Peel and chop 1 carrot, and 1 apple. Chop 1 stick of celery. Add apple juice to thin down. Whizz. Very healthy.

French Onion Soup ★★

Serves 2   Preparation time: 20 mins   Cooking time: 10 mins

French onion soup is inexpensive to make, and the caramelised onions taste delicious. You need to watch the onions as they brown and stir them frequently; but the end result is worth the effort. The cheesy croutons make a good contrast of flavour.

1 large onion, sliced
1½ tablespoons oil to fry
1½ mugs water + 1 vegetable stock cube
½ teaspoon marmite
salt and pepper

Cheesy croutons

1 slice wholemeal bread
¼ mug grated cheese

1. Heat the oil in a saucepan. Add the sliced onions. Fry on a fairly high heat for 6-8 minutes until the onions are really brown; verging on burnt. You will need to watch them carefully and stir frequently to stop them from actually burning.
2. Once the onions are really brown add the water, crumbled stock cube, and marmite. Bring to the boil, and then turn down to simmer for 10 minutes.
3. While the soup is cooking, make some cheese on toast. You will not need to butter the toast. Once toasted, cut into squares to use as croutons.
4. Taste the soup and season. Pour into a bowl and drop the croutons on top.

Tomato and Lentil Soup ★

Serves 1   Preparation time: 15 mins   Cooking time: 20 minutes

Use the hand-held blender for this recipe. If you don't have one, don't worry. It tastes just the same unblended. Make enough for 2 and eat the rest the next day.

1/4 mug red lentils
" cube butter
clove garlic, chopped
medium onion, chopped
medium carrot, chopped
x 400g can tomatoes
1 ½ mug water + 1 vegetable stock cube, crumbled in.
½ teaspoon marmite

Croutons
1 slice wholemeal bread
a little oil to fry

1. Heat the butter in a saucepan, add the onions, carrots, and garlic. Cook until the onions are soft.

2. Add the lentils, tomatoes, marmite, stock cube, and water. Bring to the boil, then turn down and simmer for 20 minutes until the lentils are tender.

3. Make the croutons while the soup is cooking. Add some oil to the frying pan, dip both sides of the bread in the oil, then fry each side for 2 minutes or so until it is browned. Cut into squares.

4. Once the soup is cooked season well with salt and freshly ground black pepper. Use a hand held blender to liquidise the soup. Serve with the croutons.

Apple and Cashew Soup ★★

Serves 2   Preparation time: 10 mins   Cooking time: 30 mins

This soup has a fresh, sweet-and-savoury taste, and it is quick and easy to make. Mak
enough for 2, and you can keep the rest for the next day. Alternatively, freeze it and kee
for a day when you are too busy to cook.

2 carrots
1 small onion
1 small potato
1 small cooking apple
oil to fry

1½ mugs water
2 vegetable stock cubes, crumbled
¼ x 100g pack of cashews, chopped
salt and pepper

1. Peel and chop the apple. Chop the rest of the vegetables, and fry in the oil using a saucepa
Allow the vegetables to brown a little.
2. Add the rest of the ingredients and bring to the boil. Simmer for 30 minutes until th
vegetables are tender.
3. Allow to cool a little, then whizz with the blender. Reheat, and season well with salt an
pepper. You don't need to put the fancy bits of apple on that you see in the photo!

Leek Soup ★★

Serves 2   Preparation time: 10 mins   Cooking time: 20 mins

This is a lovely creamy soup. Make a good quantity and once it has cooled, you can freeze it in sealed bags in your freezer drawer. The recipe asks for double cream but you can replace this with milk.

2 leeks, sliced
1 small potato, diced
1 small carrot, chopped
1" cube butter to fry
3 mugs water with 2 vegetable stock cubes crumbled in
salt and pepper to taste
2 tablespoons double cream (you can use milk)

1. Melt the butter in a saucepan and fry the vegetables for 4-5 minutes. Stir frequently.
2. Add the stock and bring to the boil. Turn down the heat and simmer for 20 minutes.
3. Using the hand-held blender, whizz until the soup is smooth.
4. Stir in the double cream and season with salt and pepper. Serve with crusty bread.

Corn Soup ★★

Serves 2   Preparation and cooking time: 20 mins

This soup has a sweet, creamy flavour. It originates in Mexico but is not spicy. It's quick and easy to make. The recipe is for 2 servings, so either share or use the next day. Use any leftover cream in a sauce (pages 20 & 21).

I pepper, red or green, cut into strips	I mug of water
I tablespoon oil to fry	I vegetable stock cube, crumbled
½ onion, chopped	I tablespoon double cream
½ x 340g can of sweetcorn	salt and pepper

1. Use a saucepan. Fry the onion and pepper in the oil until the onion is soft.
2. Add the water and stock cube, and bring to the boil. Add the sweetcorn, and simmer for 3-4 minutes.
3. Take out 3 of the strips of pepper, and keep to garnish the soup. Use the blender to whiz the soup, but do not make it too fine; keep it a bit lumpy. Stir in the cream, and season with salt and pepper.
4. Pour into a bowl and put the 3 bits of pepper on the soup. Enjoy.

Lentil & Apricot Soup ⋆

Serves 2   Preparation time: 10 mins   Cooking time: 30 mins

The ingredients here may seems a bit strange, but they taste delicious. You can cook the soup, eat half, and then freeze the other half if you like.

3 tablespoons red lentils
2 tablespoons chopped dried apricots
1 medium potato, diced
2 mugs water + 2 vegetable stock cubes, crumbled in
juice of half a lemon
1 teaspoon curry paste
1 teaspoon oregano
salt and pepper

1. Put all the ingredients, except the oregano, in a saucepan. Bring to the boil, then turn down the heat and simmer for 30 minutes.
2. Whizz with the hand held blender. Add the oregano. Reheat and serve.

Salads

As you can see from the picture below, salad is more than lettuce, tomato and cucumber. Y
can buy bags of green leaf salad from the supermarket. Don't be fooled into buying bags
lettuce; it is much cheaper to buy the lettuce whole, and all you have to do is wash it with co
water. The picture shows spring onions, fennel, red onions, baby sweetcorn, tomatoes, celer
carrots, peppers, and cucumber. You can also buy things like spinach, chicory, celeriac (whic
is eaten raw, grated, or thinly sliced), radishes, beetroot, and maybe a few other things yo
can find. All these varieties of salad provide their own little store of nutrition when eate
fresh and raw.

Salad Dressings ★ ★

I have spoken with a number of students who would like to know how to make some different salad dressings. Here are some:

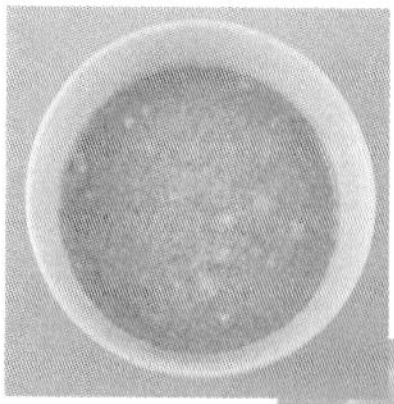

Coconut dressing

1 tablespoon oil, ½ teaspoon curry paste, ½ mug coconut cream, juice of ½ lemon, 1 teaspoon sugar, 1 tablespoon water. Mix together.

Creamy Paprika dressing

1 teaspoon sugar, 2 teaspoons paprika, 4 tablespoons white wine vinegar, 1 egg, ¾ mug olive oil. Mix everything but the oil together. Using the blender, gradually add the oil – keep whisking and the dressing should turn thick and creamy. Season with salt and pepper.

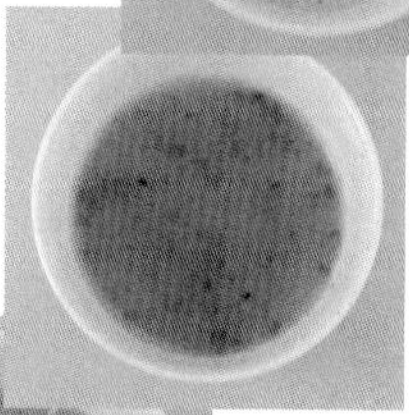

French dressing

1 teaspoon sugar, 1 teaspoon chives, juice of 1 lemon, 2 tablespoons olive oil, 1 garlic clove, chopped (optional); salt and pepper. Mix together and shake if possible.

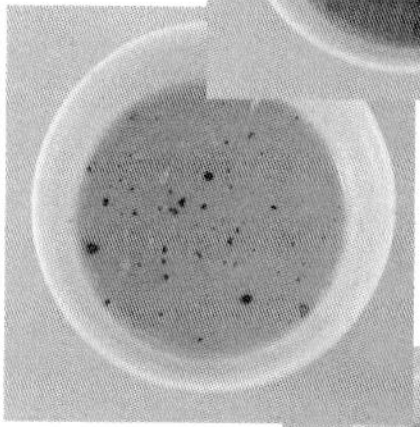

Honey and Lemon

Juice of one lemon, 2 tablespoons honey, salt and pepper. Mix together.

Peanut dressing

2 tablespoons peanut butter, ⅓ mug coconut milk, and a teaspoon tomato puree. Mix everything together.

Piquant dressing

3 tablespoons olive oil, 3 tablespoons white wine vinegar, 1 teaspoon chopped chives, 1 teaspoon paprika, 1 teaspoon soya sauce, ¼ teaspoon wholegrain mustard, 3 tablespoons water, 2 tablespoons brown sugar, salt and pepper. Mix together.

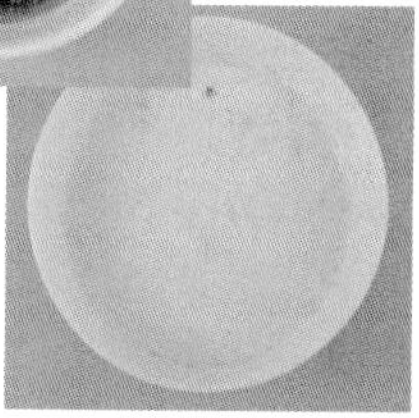

Yogurt dressing

1 small pot of natural yogurt (or 4 tablespoons), ½ teaspoon honey, grated rind and juice of a lemon, 2 spring onions (finely chopped), salt and pepper. Mix everything together.

Chick Pea and Feta Salad ★

Serves 2   Preparation time: 10 mins

Feta cheese has a lovely tangy taste, and when mixed with the chick peas and spinach, make
a delicious combination of tastes and textures. Very easy too. If you want to save half fc
the next day divide into 2 portions before adding the dressing, since it causes the greens
wilt.

I x 400g tin chick peas, rinsed and drained
½ x 200g pack of feta cheese, cut into chunks
I medium red pepper, roughly chopped
good handful of spinach

Croutons

oil to fry
I slice wholemeal bread

Choose a dressing from page 31. Make enough for 2.

1. Prepare a salad dressing from page 31. Alternatively, you can use a ready-made Frencl
dressing.
2. Make the croutons: heat oil in a frying pan, and fry the slice of bread on both sides. Cu
into small squares.
3. Sort through the spinach and discard any thick stalks, put the good spinach in a bowl.
4. Put all the ingredients together in the bowl and mix. Eat straight away because the dressing
will cause the spinach to wilt.

Sweet Potato Salad ★ ★

Serves 2   Preparation time: 15 mins

This salad is fresh tasting and full of goodness. The grated celeriac and the pecans create an unusual flavour. You can buy portions of celeriac in most supermarkets. Use any leftovers in casseroles, or roast them with other vegetables.

sweet potatoes
celery stick
mug grated celeriac
spring onion, sliced

⅓ mug pecan nuts
a few lettuce leaves
1 teaspoon chives
French dressing (page 31)

Peel and dice the sweet potato and boil for 10 minutes until tender. Drain, and set aside to cool.

Make the French dressing (page 31).

When the sweet potato has cooled, mix in the onion, celery, grated celeriac, chives, and pecans.

Put the lettuce on a plate and pile the salad on top. Drizzle the French dressing over. Eat!
Do not prepare too far in advance because the French dressing will cause the lettuce to wilt.

Pineapple Salad ★ ★

Serves 2   Preparation time: 25 mins

This is a nutty salad with a sweet twist to it. The coconut dressing is unusual and complimen
the salad well. If you want to save half for the next day remember to divide in 2 befo
adding the dressing.

½ mug of long grain rice
1 mug water, to cook rice
6 florets of broccoli
½ x 160g pack of snow peas
1 small tin of pineapple

½ mug pine nuts, toasted
¼ mug raisins

Coconut dressing (page 31)

1. Cook the rice in the water (page 11).
2. Bring half a pan of water to the boil. Add the broccoli to the boiling water, and ther
minutes later add the snow peas. Cook for another 3 minutes and both should be cooked.
3. Chop the pineapple into bite-sized pieces, and toast the pine nuts (page 7).
4. Add all the ingredients together and pour the coconut dressing over.

Apple and Bean Salad ★★

Serves 2   Preparation time: 20 mins

A yummy sweet-and-savoury combination. You can use any variety of canned beans. Always be sure to rinse them well as some of the soaking juices are not good for you.

large potatoes, diced
1 x 400g can of bortolli beans, or any other canned beans (not baked beans!)
1 red dessert apple
1 tablespoon lemon juice
1 shallot or very small onion, sliced
1 small yellow pepper, diced

Dressing

Juice of a lemon
2 tablespoons olive oil
1 dessertspoon wholegrain mustard
1 clove garlic, chopped
1 teaspoon sugar
1 teaspoon chives

Boil the diced potatoes for 10-15 minutes until they are cooked. Drain.
Peel the apple, remove the core, and chop into chunks.
Mix all the ingredients together (not the dressing ingredients).
Mix together the dressing ingredients and drizzle over the top of the salad.
Serve with green salad.

Goat's Cheese Salad ★

Serves 2   Preparation time: 10 mins   Cooking time: 6 mins

Goat's cheese is a little more expensive than most cheeses but has quite a different taste. When combined with ciabatta, it provides an interesting and delicious meal.

2 tablespoons olive oil
½ teaspoon white wine vinegar
1 teaspoon green pesto
1 ciabatta loaf
4 small tomatoes, sliced
lettuce
125g pack of goat's cheese

1. Preheat the oven to 220°C/gas mark 9.
2. Mix the oil, pesto, and wine vinegar. Stir well. Cut the bread in two, and then take one ho and cut horizontally. Leave the other half for tomorrow's sandwiches. Take the 2 halves bread, and sprinkle some of the oil and vinegar over the inside . Place the sliced tomatoes the bread.
3. Cut the goat's cheese into 6 slices, and arrange them over the bread. Brush with dressir and put in the oven for 6 minutes.
4. Pour the remaining dressing over the lettuce, and serve together with the bread ar cheese.

Sala

Mango & Noodle Salad ★ ★

Serves 2   Preparation time: 15 mins

The fruit and the peanut dressing makes this quite a quirky salad. It is best served hot, and shared with a friend since it does not reheat well. You can use the leftover mango from this recipe in a smoothie.

½ x 200g pack of ready-to-eat egg noodles
1 tablespoon oil
2 cloves garlic, chopped
½ red chilli, deseeded and chopped
2 peppers, any colour you like
½ ripe mango
3 spring onions, chopped

Dressing
2 tablespoons peanut butter
⅓ mug coconut milk
½ teaspoon tomato puree

1. Peel the mango, and slice off the main sections, cutting around the stone. Cut into strips.
2. Make the dressing: just mix the ingredients together; you can heat them if you wish.
3. Heat the oil in a frying pan. Fry the onions, garlic, peppers, and chilli for 4-5 minutes. The onions should be softened.
4. Add the mango and the noodles. Cook for 3-4 minutes, stirring frequently. Once everything is heated through, transfer to serving plates, and pour the peanut sauce over the top.

Nut & Carrot Coleslaw ★

Serves 2   Preparation time: 15 mins

You can eat this with other salads or with baked potatoes and cheese. It is so much better than any coleslaw you might buy ready-made from a supermarket. You will, of course, be eating all the vegetables fresh. If you want to keep half for the next day, divide in 2 before you put the dressing on. Keep in a sealed container and add the rest of the dressing the next day.

I carrot, grated
3 spring onions, cut into long strips
2 celery sticks, chopped
⅛ small hard white cabbage (you could use Chinese cabbage if you wish)
I tablespoon chives

3 tablespoons olive oil
½ mug cashew nuts
2 tablespoons white wine vinegar
salt and pepper
I teaspoon sugar

1. Mix together the oil, chives, wine vinegar, sugar, and salt and pepper.
2. Put all the other ingredients in a bowl and mix with a spoon. Pour over the dressing and ▶

Spicy Fruit'nut Salad ★★

Serves 2 - 3   Preparation and cooking time: 25 mins

This salad has lots of healthy things in it. It has a delicious crunchy, sweet-and-savoury flavour. You can eat it as a snack by itself, or to accompany vegetarian sausages or bean burgers.

¾ mug basmati rice, cooked in 1½ mugs water with 1 teaspoon pilau rice seasoning
oil to fry
1 medium onion, chopped
grated rind of 1 lemon
1 tablespoon tumeric
1 teaspoon curry paste

½ mug pine nuts
½ mug dates, chopped
½ mug ready-to-eat figs, chopped
2 sticks celery, chopped
4 heaped tablespoons mayonnaise
juice of a lemon
½ mug pecan nuts, roughly chopped

Cook the rice with the pilau rice seasoning.
2. Fry the onions until they begin to brown. Add the tumeric and curry paste, and mix well. Cook for 2-3 minutes. Add the rest of the ingredients and mix.

Salads

Spaghetti Bolognese ★ ★

Serves 2   Preparation and cooking time: 30 mins

There is almost nothing but vegetables in this recipe. If you want to vary it, you can add half a teaspoon of marmite or HP sauce.

I small onion, chopped
I small carrot, finely chopped
I celery stick
½ red pepper, chopped
I tablespoon olive oil, for frying
2 tablespoons red lentils

I x 400g can chopped tomatoes
I mug water + I vegetable stock cube, crumbled
I teaspoon oregano
2 portions of spaghetti to serve
grated parmesan or cheddar cheese to serve

1. Finely chop all the vegetables, and fry with the oil in a saucepan for 3-4 minutes.
2. Add the lentils, tomatoes, oregano, stock cube, and water. Bring to the boil. Season with salt and pepper. Leave to simmer for about 20 minutes until all the vegetables are cooked.
3. In the meantime, put the spaghetti on to cook (page 11).
4. When everything is cooked, drain the pasta and serve the bolognese mixture on the top. Grate some parmesan or cheddar over the top as well.

Vegetable Lasagna * * * * *

Serves 2 - 3   Preparation time: 25 mins   Cooking time: 30-35 mins

Lasagna is good for feeding large numbers of people.   Just multiply these ingredients accordingly. You can obviously vary the vegetables you use.   Any root vegetables will need to be pre-cooked.

I small onion, chopped
I clove garlic, chopped
I mushroom, sliced
I small courgette, sliced
½ red pepper, sliced
I stick celery, sliced

I x 400g tin chopped tomatoes
oil to fry
I teaspoon mixed herbs
2 x quick cheese sauce (page 20)
6 lasagna sheets
½ mug grated cheddar cheese

1. Preheat the oven to 170°C/gas mark 5.
2. Fry the onion, garlic, peppers, mushroom, celery, and courgette in the oil for 4-5 minutes. Add the tin of tomatoes and bring to the boil. Simmer for 5 minutes.
3. Make the double quantity of quick cheese sauce (page 20).
4. Put half the vegetable mixture in the bottom of a casserole dish. Cover with one layer of lasagna strips. Pour half the cheese sauce over. Cover with another layer of lasagna strips. Put the rest of the vegetables on top. Cover with another layer of lasagna strips. Pour the rest of the cheese sauce over. Top with the grated cheese.
5. Cook in the oven for 25-30 minutes. Test the pasta to see if it is cooked, if not, turn the oven down to 160°C/gas mark 4, and cook for another 5-10 minutes. Serve with salad and garlic bread.

Cannelloni ★ ★ ★ ★ ★

Serves 2   Preparation time: 30 mins   Cooking time: 25 mins

This is dinner party food. It is so fiddly to fill the cannelloni shells, hence the 5 ★ ★ ★ ★ rating. It is well worth the effort. Italian in origin; excellent food; bound to impress any gues...

Oil to fry
½ x onion, chopped
I clove garlic, chopped
handfull of spinach, torn into large pieces
300g pack of cream cheese, or ricotta cheese
2 tablespoons grated parmesan

8 cannelloni shells
2 extra tablespoons grated parmesan f...
sprinkling on top.
I quantity of tomato sauce (page 21)
(You could use the quick cheese sauce ...
page 20 instead of the tomato sauce.)

1. Preheat the oven to 180°C/gas mark 6.
2. Make the tomato sauce (page 21).
3. Heat the oil in a frying pan, and fry the onion and garlic until the onions are soft. Add th... spinach and cook until it wilts; approximately I minute.
4. Mix the cream cheese and parmesan together in a bowl, and soften with a fork. Add th... onion and spinach mixture. Mix. Use this mixture to fill the cannelloni shells. Spoon into th... top of the cannelloni tubes and push in with the handle of a small spoon. Repeat the proces... until the shell is completely full. Your hands will get very messy.
5. Place in a greased casserole dish or shallow ovenproof dish; and cover with the tomat... sauce, or the quick cheese sauce. Cook in the oven for 15 minutes. Sprinkle the rest of th... parmesan over the top and cook for another 10 minutes. Serve immediately.

Pasta & Pepper Sauce ★★

Serves 2   Preparation and cooking time: 30mins

This very simple, tasty sauce is ideal to make the quantity for 2 and either share it or keep it for a few days time. This is a good snack meal. You could add a few fried vegetables, such as mushrooms, peppers, or courgettes if you wish.

1 red pepper, deseeded, and cut in half
1 red chilli, chopped
2 tomatoes, chopped into pieces
1 clove garlic, whole

2 tablespoons oil
1 teaspoon oregano
2 portions of pasta

1. Preheat the oven to 180°C/gas mark 6. Place the peppers, tomatoes, and garlic on a baking sheet and brush with the oil. Roast for 20 minutes.
2. Put the pasta on to cook.
3. Once roasted, put the peppers, tomatoes, chilli, garlic, and oregano in a bowl and whizz with the hand held blender. Warm the sauce through again.
4. When the pasta is cooked, drain, and put on plates. Pour the sauce over the top.
5. If you want to add vegetables to this, simply chop them up, fry them in a frying pan, and add the sauce and mix together.

Pasta with Broccoli ★

Serves 1   Preparation time: 15 mins

This is a very good all-in-one meal. Pasta, broccoli, and pine nuts provide a fairly balanced meal. It is also quick and easy to make.

1 portion of pasta (penne is shown in the photo)
about ½ a head of broccoli, broken into small 'trees'
1 tablespoon pine nuts
1 tablespoon green pesto
grated parmesan for the top
1 dessertspoon olive oil

1. Cook the pasta (page 11).
2. When the pasta has 5 minutes left to cook add the broccoli to the saucepan.
3. Drain the pasta and broccoli when cooked.
4. Mix the pesto paste with a little olive oil, and mix into the pasta along with the pine nuts.
5. Sprinkle the parmesan over the top, and serve.

Spaghetti with Beans ★

Serves 2   Preparation and cooking time: 15 mins

Very easy, very tasty, and very quick. If you freeze half the sauce and beans you will have a ready made meal for another day.

1 tablespoon oil to fry	1 mushroom, sliced
1 clove garlic, chopped	1 teaspoon oregano
½ x 400g can chopped tomatoes	½ x 310g can cannellini beans, rinsed, and drained
½ mug water	12-15 black olives
½ teaspoon sugar	1 portion of spaghetti (page 11)

1. Put spaghetti on to cook.
2. Heat oil in a frying pan. Fry garlic for 30 seconds, add the mushrooms, and cook for 1 minute.
3. Add the rest of the ingredients, and cook for 4-5 minutes on a fairly high heat. Stir continuously.
4. Drain the pasta, and put onto a plate. Pour the bean mixture over the top. Eat!

Mushroom and Brie Pasta ★★

Serves 1   Preparation and cooking time: 15-20 mins

Quick and easy to make but very tasty! Brie is, of course, a little more expensive than the usual cheddar but will add variety to your diet. Any excess will make a delicious sandwich if you add some salad to it.

¼ x 250g pack of Brie, cut into slices
1" cube butter
2 spring onions, chopped
6 medium mushrooms, sliced
1 clove of garlic, finely chopped
1 teaspoon wholegrain mustard

3 tablespoons cream
2-3 pieces sun-dried tomatoes, sliced
½ vegetable stock cube crumbled into 2 tablespoons water
1 mug of pasta, cooked (page 11)

1. Heat butter in a frying pan. Fry the spring onions, garlic, and mushrooms until the mushrooms are soft.
2. Add the stock cube and water, and simmer, uncovered, until almost all the stock has reduced.
3. Add the tomatoes, mustard, cream, and cheese. Cook until the Brie has melted.
4. Stir in the cooked pasta, and serve.

Pasta with Roast Veg ★ ★

Serves 2   Preparation time: 15 mins   Cooking time: 30 mins

This is a quick way to make a delicious meal. Roasting vegetables is so easy, and creates a delicious flavour as the starches in the vegetables caramelise. (See page 13 for roasting other vegetables.)

½ onion, cut into wedges
I courgette, cut into wedges
I clove garlic, chopped
I tablespoon oil to roast

3-4 cherry tomatoes
2 mushrooms, sliced
salt and pepper
I portion of pasta

1. Preheat the oven to 190°C/gas mark 7.
2. Put the onion, courgette, and chopped garlic on a baking tray. Sprinkle on the oil, and some salt and pepper. Toss the vegetables in the oil and seasoning so it is evenly distributed.
3. Roast in the oven for 15 minutes, and then add the tomatoes and the mushrooms. Turn everything over with the slotted turner. Roast for another 15 minutes.
4. 15 minutes from the end of the roasting time, cook the pasta (page 11).
5. Drain the pasta and take the cooked vegetables out of the oven. With a slotted turner, take the vegetables off the tray and put them into the pasta. Mix and serve.

Pasta with Onions and Beans ★★★

Serves 1   Preparation and cooking time: 30 mins

The preparation time here is a bit lengthy, but not too difficult. The final result is a lovely sweet-and-sour flavour not usually associated with pasta dishes.

oil to fry
1 red onion, sliced
2 tablespoons water
2 tablespoons sugar
2 tablespoons red or white wine vinegar

1 tablespoon raisins
a handful of green beans, about 20
1 garlic clove, chopped
1 handful of spinach
one portion of tagliatelle

1. Cook the beans in boiling water until tender. This should take about 10 minutes.
2. While the beans are cooking, fry the onions in the oil in a frying pan on a medium heat, for about 10 minutes. Stir frequently. They should be soft and quite brown. Add the water, raisins, sugar, and vinegar, and cook for 2-3 minutes. Take this mixture out of the frying pan, set aside. Wash the pan.
3. The beans should be cooked now. Take them out of the pan and put with the onion mixture. Put the pasta on to cook (page 11).
4. Fry the garlic in oil for 1 minute. Add the spinach, and cook until it begins to wilt. Add the beans and onion mixture back to the pan, and mix.
5. The pasta should be cooked by now. Drain and put on a plate. Top with the onions and beans.

Pasta and Rice

Roast Tomatoes and Spaghetti ★

Serves 1   Preparation time: 5 mins   Cooking time: 15 mins

The sharp taste of the feta cheese and the roast tomatoes in this dish are a yummy combination.

8-10 cherry tomatoes
oil to roast
1 portion of spaghetti
⅓ x 200g block of feta cheese, cut into chunks

1 teaspoon chives
12-15 olives
grated parmesan cheese (optional)

1. Preheat the oven to 180°C/gas mark 6.
2. Put the tomatoes in an ovenproof dish and drizzle olive oil over them. Season with salt and pepper. Put them in the hot oven to roast for 15 minutes.
3. In the meantime, put the spaghetti on to cook (See page 11).
4. Drain the pasta, and return to the pan with the olives, feta cheese, and chives. When the tomatoes are cooked, tip them and the juices from the bottom of the dish, into the pan. Mix together, and serve.

Broccoli & Tomato Spaghetti ★★

Serves 1   Preparation time: 20 mins

This pasta dish is clean, fresh, and tasty. It does not have a sauce, as such, but the vegetables are very moist.

1 portion of spaghetti (page 11)
6 small florets of broccoli
1 tablespoon olive oil, for frying
½ onion, finely chopped
1 small clove garlic, chopped

2 sun-dried tomatoes, cut into slices
2 tomatoes, cut into chunks
salt and pepper
grated parmesan to serve

1. Put the spaghetti in a pan of boiling water. Cook for 5 minutes. Add the broccoli florets, and cook for a further 5 minutes. By this time both should be cooked.
2. While the pasta is cooking, fry the onions and garlic in a frying pan. Cook for 3-4 minutes until the onion begins to brown. Add the tomatoes and sun-dried tomatoes. Cook on a lower heat for another 4-5 minutes. Stir occasionally. Season well with salt and pepper.
3. Drain the pasta and broccoli, and mix everything together in the frying pan. This way you will pick up the juices from the frying pan. Serve immediately, and top with parmesan if you wish.

Spaghetti with Red Pesto ⭐

Serves 1   Preparation time: 20 mins

Very quick and easy to make, and also full of flavour. You can obviously add different vegetables to the sauce: green beans, mange tout, sugar snaps, etc.

1 portion of spaghetti
1 tomato, cut into chunks
1 mushroom, sliced
½ onion, chopped
½ red pepper, cut into chunks

½ x 190g jar red pesto
2 tablespoons pine nuts
2 tablespoons cream
oil to fry

1. Cook the spaghetti (page 11).
2. Fry the onion, pepper, and mushroom for 2-3 minutes in a frying pan. Add the tomato, and cook for 1-2 minutes.
3. Add the pesto, cream, and pine nuts, and heat through.
4. Drain the spaghetti and serve the sauce on top.

Risotto ★★

Serves 1   Preparation time: 10 mins   Cooking time: 25-30 mins

Risotto is a very versatile recipe. The instructions below give you the basic idea, and then you can experiment and add different ingredients yourself. Arborio rice is the best to use for risotto but you can use long grain or other varieties.

½ onion, chopped
2 mushrooms, sliced
1 clove of garlic, chopped
1 leek, sliced
½ courgette, cut into small pieces.
1½ mugs water
1 vegetable stock cube
½ mug rice
1 tablespoon pine nuts
salt and pepper

1. Fry the onions and garlic for 2 minutes. Add the rice, and fry for another minute.
2. Add the water, crumbled stock cube, leeks, courgette, and mushrooms. Bring to the boil, and season well with salt and pepper.
3. Simmer with the lid on the pan for 25-30 minutes, until the rice is tender and the liquid is almost gone. Risotto should not be really dry. Don't allow all the liquid to boil away. Add more liquid if necessary.
4. Add the pine nuts at the end of the cooking time.

Variations

Here are a few ideas for variations on the basic risotto recipe. If you are using vegetables which cook in a short time, they need to be added towards the end of the cooking time. Broccoli is not great in risotto because it tends to break up and go mushy. These variations begin at stage 2 of the basic recipe. So, always begin with the onions, garlic, and rice and water.

You can use frozen or tinned vegetables in these recipes if you like.

Green veg risotto

At stage 2, add a vegetable stock cube; green beans, cut into pieces; peas; and broad beans. At the end of the cooking time, add some spinach and cook until it wilts. Serve topped with parmesan.

Spicy pumpkin

At stage 2, add I small deseeded chilli, chopped; a vegetable stock cube; pieces of pumpkin; half a courgette, chopped; and 2 sliced mushrooms. Top with grated cheddar cheese; it will melt into the risotto. Don't try to cook the cheese or stir it in.

Green pepper and sweetcorn

At stage 2, add half a green pepper, roughly chopped, and a sliced mushroom. 5 minutes before the end of the cooking time add a small tin of sweetcorn, and a tablespoon cashew nuts.

Spicy bean

At stage 2, add I tablespoon black eyed beans, either tinned or soaked (page 7); I carrot, chopped; I small courgette, chopped; 2 teaspoons curry paste; and some chives.

Mexican

At stage 2, replace I mug of water with half a 400g tin of chopped tomatoes. Also add, I chopped red pepper; I deseeded red chilli, chopped; half a tin of chick peas; and a teaspoon sugar. Serve topped with grated cheddar cheese, or with soured cream.

Spanish

At stage 2, replace the I mug of water with half a 400g tin of chopped tomatoes. Also add 2 sliced mushrooms, and half a chopped red pepper. 5 minutes before the end, add 6-8 olives. Serve topped with a fried egg.

Split Pea Risotto ★ ★

Serves 2   Preparation time: 15 mins   Cooking time: 1 hour

You need to plan in advance for this one, since the split peas need soaking overnight, and the cooking time is quite long. Split peas do not microwave well; so if you are reheating any leftovers, you will need to do it in a saucepan. You may need to add a little water to do so.

⅓ mug yellow split peas
1 tablespoon olive oil
1 medium onion, chopped
1 clove garlic, chopped
2 teaspoon curry paste
2 tomatoes, chopped

1 medium potato, diced
¼ mug long grain rice
1 mug water
1 vegetable stock cube
juice of ½ lemon
1 teaspoon coriander

1. Drain the peas, and rinse.
2. Heat the oil in a saucepan. Fry the onions, garlic, potato, and tomatoes. Cook for 2-3 minutes.
3. Add the rice, water, crumbled stock cube, curry paste, and the peas. Bring to the boil, and then turn down to simmer. Cover with the lid, and cook for 1 hour. Check every now and then to make sure it is not boiling dry. If it gets dry, add a little more water.
4. Once everything is cooked add the lemon juice and coriander. Stir. There should not be too much liquid left. If so, simmer for about 5 minutes without the lid on the pan to reduce the liquid.

Cheesy Rice Slice ★ ★

Serves 2   Preparation time: 15 mins   Cooking time: 25 mins

This is a bit like quiche without the bother of pastry. It is good to eat either hot or cold; therefore, ideal to make on one day, and eat the rest the next day.

½ mug long grain rice, cooked
handfull spinach
1 tablespoon oil to fry
1 small red onion
1 mug cheddar cheese

2 eggs, beaten
2 tablespoons cream
2 tomatoes, sliced
½ mug grated cheese for the top

1. Preheat the oven to 180°C/gas mark 6. Cook the rice (page 11).
2. Heat the oil in a frying pan, and fry the onions. Once they begin to go soft, add the spinach and cook for 30 seconds or so, until it begins to wilt. Take off the heat.
3. Add the cooked rice, cheese, cream, and beaten eggs. Stir well.
4. Pour into a greased casserole dish. Arrange the sliced tomatoes on the top. Sprinkle the grated cheese evenly over the top.
5. Cook in the oven for 25 minutes. The cheese should be brown.

Sweet and Spicy Pilau **

Serves 2   Preparation and cooking time: 30 mins

This is an appetizing rice salad; full of good things. Good to eat on its own as a snack, c
with some green salad. Will keep in the fridge for 2-3 days.

2 tablespoons oil, to fry
1 onion, sliced
½ teaspoon chilli powder
½ mug basmati rice
1½ mugs water

¼ mug currants
¼ mug ready-to-eat apricots, chopped
¼ mug sultanas, currants, or raisins
¼ mug pine nuts or almonds

1. Fry the onions in a saucepan until they become caramelised (go quite brown).
2. Add the rice, water, and chilli powder. Bring to the boil; then turn down to simmer for abou.
10-15 minutes, uncovered, until the rice is cooked and the water has been absorbed.
3. Take off the heat and stir in the fruit and nuts. Leave to stand.

Tomato and Rice

Serves 2   Preparation time: 10 mins   Cooking time: 5 mins

This is a good way to use leftover rice. It makes an easy and inexpensive meal. Use mature cheddar in order to give the topping a kick. Serve with salad.

1 tablespoon oil	1 x 400g can chopped tomatoes
1 small onion, sliced	½ mug grated cheddar cheese
½ red or green pepper, chopped	½ teaspoon basil
1 small clove garlic	1 stock cube
½ mug long grain rice, cooked	½ tin sweetcorn
1 mushroom, sliced	

1. Fry the onion, garlic, peppers, and mushrooms in the oil, in a frying pan. Cook for 3-4 minutes until they begin to go soft.
2. Add the rice, crumbled stock cube, tomatoes, sweetcorn, and basil. Mix together, and cook for 3-4 minutes until everything is thoroughly heated through.
3. Grate the cheese over the top, and put under a hot grill until the cheese begins to brown.
4. Serve with some salad.

Khitcherie ★ ★ ★

Serves 2   Preparation and cooking time: 30 mins   Soaking time: 1 hour

This is an original Indian dish which developed into Colonial Kedgeree when fish was added. Here it has the spilt peas and nuts to provide the protein etc. It can be eaten on its own or as a rice dish with other things. You can vary the amount of curry paste to your taste.

½ mug split peas
2 tablespoons oil to fry
½ onion, chopped
1 clove garlic, chopped
1 fresh chilli, chopped
1 teaspoon grated fresh ginger

2 teaspoons curry paste
1 mug basmati rice
½ mug raisins
1½ mugs water
½ mug toasted cashews, roughly chopped

1. Put the split peas in a bowl and cover with cold water. Soak for 1 hour.
2. Heat the oil in a saucepan and add the onions, garlic, chilli, and ginger. Stir frequently and cook for 2-3 minutes.
3. Add the rice, drained split peas, water, raisins, and curry paste. Bring to the boil, then turn down to simmer for 15 minutes, or until the rice is cooked. The liquid should have almost boiled away. If not, allow to cook a little more. The mixture should not be very dry; if it is, add a little more water. Take off the heat and stir in the toasted cashews. Serve with yogurt.

Classic Nut Roast ★ ★

Serves 2   Preparation time: 10 mins   Cooking time: 20 mins

You can use a variety of nuts in this recipe, but cashews, macadamia, or brazil nuts seem to work the best. They have a slightly sweeter taste than some other nuts. Any leftovers are ideal to keep for the next day. You can eat either hot or cold.

1 small onion, chopped finely
1 x 200g pack chopped cashew nuts
2 mushrooms, chopped finely
2 slices wholemeal bread
½ mug water + a vegetable stock cube
1 teaspoon marmite
1 teaspoon mixed herbs

Serve with salad, baked potatoes, pasta, or roasted vegetables.

Also, if you wish, serve with one of the sauces on pages 20 & 21.

1. Preheat the oven to 180°C/gas mark 6. Grease a small ovenproof dish - you can use your casserole dish.
2. Fry the onions in a little oil in a saucepan until they begin to brown. Add the mushrooms, and cook for a further 2-3 minutes. Take off the heat.
3. Add the chopped nuts to the pan.
4. Make the bread into breadcrumbs. Just rub it between your fingers; it does not matter if the breadcrumbs are a bit chunky. Add to the pan.
5. Add ½ vegetable stock cube into ½ a mug of boiling water to make up the stock. Add the teaspoon of marmite and stir until dissolved.
6. Add the contents of the mug to the pan, along with the herbs. Mix everything together.
7. Pour into the dish and cook for 20 minutes in the oven. If you double the quantity, you will need to cook for another 5 minutes. The nuts should be brown on top.

Bubble & Squeak ★★

Serves 2   Preparation and cooking time: 30 mins

A simple, old-fashioned recipe, with a little more than potato and cabbage to it.

I medium potato, diced
½ small squash, cut into chunks
I small carrot, chopped
I small onion, chopped
½ mug frozen peas
I mug shredded cabbage
I dessertspoon chives
oil to fry
½ mug toasted cashews,
roughly chopped
½ mug grated cheese
salt and pepper

1. Boil the carrots for 5 minutes in a saucepan, then add the squash and potatoes, and boil for another 5 minutes. Add the peas and cabbage, and boil for a further 5 minutes. Drain the vegetables.
2. Turn the grill on to heat up.
3. Fry the onion in a frying pan for 3-4 minutes until it begins to brown. Add the rest of the vegetables and the chives. Fry for 2-3 minutes, stirring frequently. Season well.
4. Sprinkle the top with the grated cheese and the cashews. Place the frying pan under the grill until the cheese is browned.
5. Serve with tomato sauce (page 20 & 21).

Potato & Nut Terrine ★ ★ ★

Serves 4   Preparation time: 25 mins   Cooking time: 50-55 mins

This is a really delicious nut roast. Serve with baked potatoes, salads, or one of the sauces on page 20 & 21. The recipe serves 4, but you can eat it hot or cold, so it's OK to have for lunches and snacks for a few days. It is served here with Mango and noodle salad (page 37).

2 medium potatoes, diced
200g pack of pecan nuts, roughly chopped
200g pack of cashew nuts, roughly chopped
I red onion, chopped
2 cloves garlic, chopped
4-5 mushrooms, chopped

2 tablespoons butter
I tablespoon curry paste
4 eggs, beaten
½ x 250g pack of cream cheese, softened
½ mug grated parmesan
Serve with a sauce, or salad

I. Preheat the oven to 170°C/gas mark 5. Grease a loaf tin, and put a piece of greaseproof paper across the bottom.
2. Cook the potatoes in boiling water for 10 minutes. Drain, and mash slightly with a fork. It does not need to be smooth.
3. Fry the onions, garlic, and mushrooms in the butter for 4-5 minutes, until they are softened. Add the curry paste and stir well. Add this to the potatoes in the saucepan, along with the eggs, cream cheese, nuts, and parmesan. Season well and mix together.
4. Put the mixture into the loaf tin and bake in the oven for 50-55 minutes. Serve hot or cold with tomato sauce (page 20 & 21), or a salad.

Nuts and Beans

Nut & Courgette Slice ★ ★

Serves 2   Preparation time: 15 mins   Cooking time: 40 mins

This roast has a delightful, subtle, nutty flavour. It is served here with salad and a yogu
dressing (page 31).

I mug roughly chopped nuts, any variety
oil to fry
I clove garlic, chopped
I small onion, chopped
2 eggs, beaten,
2 tablespoons milk

I slice bread made into breadcrumbs (page
I large courgette, grated
I small carrot, grated
½ mug grated cheddar cheese
salt and pepper

1. Preheat the oven to 180°C/gas mark 6. Grease a loaf tin and put a piece of greaseproc
paper on the bottom.
2. Fry the onion and garlic in a saucepan for 2-3 minutes. Add the rest of the ingredients an
mix well.
3. Pour into the loaf tin. Bake in the oven for 35-40 minutes until browned on top.
4. Make sure the sides are loosened from the loaf tin, and tip out. Once cooled, serve slice
with salad and a dressing.

Nut and Tomato Roast ★ ★ ★

Serves 2   Preparation time: 20 mins   Cooking time: 25 mins

This is a scrumptious nut loaf, it takes a little more time to prepare but it's worth it for something a little different. The tomato sauce is unusual, try it. You can eat this hot or cold.

1 large potato, diced
1 tablespoon oil
1 small onion, chopped
1 clove garlic, chopped
½ mug mixed nuts, chopped
1 slice granary or wholemeal bread, made into crumbs
½ teaspoon chives or coriander
¼ mug water + 1 vegetable stock cube, crumbled
1 egg
3 medium mushrooms, chopped

4 pieces of sun-dried tomato, sliced
salt and pepper

Tomato sauce

3 tablespoons creme frais
1 teaspoon tomato puree
1 teaspoon honey
½ teaspoon coriander or basil
1 teaspoon chives

1. Preheat the oven to 170°C/gas mark 5. Grease a loaf tin.
2. Cook the potato in boiling water for about 10-15 minutes until it is cooked. Drain and mash a little with a fork.
3. Heat the oil in a frying pan, and cook the onion and garlic for 3-4 minutes. In a bowl, mix together the potatoes, nuts, breadcrumbs, stock, water, chives, and egg. Season with salt and pepper.
4. Fry the mushrooms in the frying pan until they begin to brown.
5. Spread half the potato and nut mixture evenly into the bottom of the loaf tin. Place the sun-dried tomatoes and mushrooms over the top, spread evenly. Add the rest of the potato mixture to make the top layer. Cook for 25 minutes in the oven.
6. To make the tomato sauce simply mix all the ingredients together.

Nuts and Beans

Nutty Veg Crumble ★★★

Serves 2-3   Preparation time: 20 mins   Cooking time: 30 mins

The topping here is more than just 'crumble', it also has nuts and cheese in it. You can vary the vegetables as you wish. Add the quicker cooking vegetables (broccoli for example), towards the end of the boiling time.

oil to fry
1 sweet potato (you may use normal ones)
1 parsnip
1 carrot
1 onion
¼ swede
1 x 400g tin chopped tomatoes
½ mug water + 1 vegetable stock cube

Crumble topping
⅕ x 250g block butter
¾ mug plain flour, or equal proportions of buckwheat and plain flour
½ mug grated cheddar cheese
½ mug nuts, chopped (use any variety; pine nuts, or cashews work well)

1. Preheat the oven to 170°C/gas mark 5.
2. Chop the vegetables into bite size chunks. Heat the oil in a saucepan and fry the vegetables for 4-5 minutes. Stir frequently. Allow them to brown a little.
3. Add the tomatoes, water, and crumbled vegetable stock cube, and bring to the boil. Turn down the heat and simmer for 10 minutes, or until they are tender.
4. While the vegetables are cooking, put the flour and butter in a bowl, and rub in the butter using your finger ends and thumbs. The mixture should resemble breadcrumbs. Add the cheese and nuts. Mix together.
5. When the vegetables are cooked, pour them into the bottom of a casserole dish. Sprinkle the crumble mixture, evenly, over the top. Press down gently to compact the crumble.
6. Cook in the oven for 25-30 minutes.

Nuts and Beans

Chick Pea Patties ★ ★ ★

erves 2   Preparation and cooking time: 25 mins

ickpeas are an important source of protein. Serve with salad, yogurt dressing and spicy
ions. They are yummy together. Don't fry any patties you may want to keep until the next
y, but keep them covered in the fridge.

0g tin of chickpeas, rinsed and drained
grated onion
all courgette, grated
easpoon chives
gg
lice of wholemeal bread
to fry

Yogurt dressing
3 tablespoons natural yogurt
I tablespoon mango or fruit chutney
I teaspoon mint

Spicy onions
I tablespoon oil
I large onion, sliced
I teaspoon curry paste

Mash the drained chick peas with a fork. It does not matter if there are a few whole ones in
ere.

Grate the onion and squeeze out the moisture from it. Mix together in a bowl with the
urgette and chick peas.

Crumble the slice of bread, beat the egg, and mix them together in a separate bowl or mug.
is helps the bread to soak and mix more easily with the other ingredients. Mix everything
gether. The mixture should be fairly stiff. Tip out onto a surface and, with floured hands,
m 4 patties.

Heat the oil in a frying pan, and put the patties in to fry. Keep the heat moderate and cook
r about 5 minutes each side.

While they are cooking make the yogurt dressing. Simply mix the ingredients together.

To make the spicy onions, fry the sliced onions in a saucepan on a fairly high heat. Allow
em to brown then add the curry paste and mix well. Cook for I minute and then take off the
at.

Split Pea Casserole ★ ★

Serves 2   Preparation time: 15 mins   Cooking time: 1 hour

This is a real winter warmer. The sweetness of the butternut squash, contrasts well with t
curry flavour. You need to decide on this one ahead of time, since the peas need to
soaked, and the cooking time is lengthy. The actual labour time is not. You can reheat a
leftovers the next day.

1 tablespoon oil, to fry	⅓ mug yellow split peas, soaked overnight
1 teaspoon wholegrain mustard	1 x 400g tin of chopped tomatoes
1 small onion, chopped	1 mug of water + 2 vegetable stock cubes
1 clove of garlic, chopped	½ a butternut squash
1 small carrot, grated	1 courgette
1 teaspoon grated ginger	1 teaspoon chopped chives
1 small red chilli, deseeded and chopped	1 teaspoon curry paste
1 dessertspoon tomato puree	salt and pepper

1. Heat the oil in a saucepan. Add the onion, ginger, garlic, and carrots. Cook for about
minutes until soft.
2. Add the peas, mustard, chilli, curry paste, tomato puree, tinned tomatoes, water, a
crumbled stock cubes. Bring to the boil and season well. Turn the heat down and simmer f
about 40 minutes.
3. Add the squash and the courgette, and simmer for a further 20 minutes until the squash
tender. Stir the chives in right at the end.
4. Eat whilst still warm with naan bread or rice.

Nuts and Bea

Chick Pea Frittata ★ ★ ★

Serves 2   Preparation and cooking time: 20 mins

Frittata is basically an omelette with loads of stuff in it. This gives some idea of how to make it. You can vary the things you put in; different varieties of beans would work well in this recipe.

1 tablespoon olive oil, to fry
1 onion, finely chopped
1 small clove garlic, chopped
1 x 400g can of chick peas, well rinsed
and drained
1 tomato, chopped
3 eggs, beaten
1 teaspoon oregano

1 tablespoon chives
½ mug grated cheese

Salsa
1 medium avocado, chopped
1 small red onion, thinly sliced
2 tomatoes, chopped
½ teaspoon chilli powder

To make up the salsa, mix the ingredients together and leave to stand while you make the frittata. See page 88 for different salsas.
   Fry the onion and garlic in a frying pan. Cook until the onion is soft.
   Turn the grill on to heat up.
   Add the peas and tomato to the frying pan, and mix. Add the herbs to the beaten eggs, and pour into the frying pan over the bean mixture. Don't stir the frittata. Cook on a medium heat for about 5 minutes until the egg begins to set. It does not need to be completely set. Sprinkle the grated cheese over the top of the frittata, and place under a hot grill for about 5 minutes, until the cheese is browned and the eggs are set.
   Serve with the salsa or one of the sauces on pages 20 & 21.

Potato Hash ★ ★

Serves 1   Preparation and cooking time: 25 mins

This is a good way to liven-up a potato and half a tin of beans. Serve with tomato ketchup or HP sauce.

2 medium potatoes
½ 400g tin baked beans
½ mug grated cheddar cheese

1. Dice the potatoes, and boil for about 10 minutes until they are cooked. Drain, return to the pan, and squash them a little with a fork. Do not mash them.
2. Stir in the beans.
3. Heat some oil in a frying pan and tip the mixture in. Don't stir, allow it to fry and brown on the bottom. Once browned, using a slotted turner, stir all the browned bits up from the bottom, leave again to allow the rest to brown. Stir in the browned bits again.
4. Serve on a plate, and put the grated cheese on the top whilst it is still hot, so that it melts. Add some ketchup.

Nuts and Beans

Lentil Bake ★ ★

Serves 2   Preparation time: 30 mins   Cooking time: 25-30 mins

Lentils, under a crunchy, cheese and potato top. You have the option of adding tofu to the base if you wish.

3 medium potatoes, diced
1" cube butter for the potatoes
½ mug red lentils
oil to fry
1 leek, sliced
1 clove garlic, chopped

1 celery stick, chopped
3-4 broccoli florets
½ x 350g pack tofu, cut into cubes (optional)
2 tablespoons pine nuts
2 teaspoons tomato puree
½ mug grated cheese
salt and pepper

1. Preheat the oven to 180°C/gas mark 6.
2. Boil the potatoes for 5 minutes, then add the broccoli and boil for a further 5 minutes. Drain. Take the broccoli out and set aside. Add some butter to the potatoes and shake them in the pan. Set to one side.
3. Boil the lentils for 15-20 minutes until they are tender, then drain.
4. Fry the leeks, garlic, and celery in a frying pan for 3-4 minutes, until they begin to brown. Add the tomato puree, lentils, pine nuts, tofu (optional), and the broccoli. Mix well, season with salt and pepper, then pour into a greased casserole dish. Put the potatoes on the top, and sprinkle with the grated cheese.
5. Bake in the oven for 25-30 minutes until the cheese is browned.
6. Serve with tomato sauce (page 20 & 21).

Channa Dhal ★

Serves 2-3   Preparation and cooking time: 15 mins

This is a traditional Bengali recipe, and, like so many Asian recipes, now quite commonplace our Western culture and kitchens. This dish makes a meal in itself, or can be eaten wit bread, naan bread, rice, or jacket potatoes.

I x 400g tin of chick peas
I tablespoon vegetable oil, to fry
I small onion, finely chopped
½ teaspoon fresh ginger
2 cloves garlic, chopped finely

I heaped dessertspoon curry paste
½ x 400g can tomatoes
2 tablespoons coconut milk
salt and pepper

I. Heat the oil in a frying pan, and fry the onions until they begin to brown. Stir frequentl
Once brown, add the ginger, curry paste, and garlic. Cook for I minute.
2. Add the tomatoes, coconut milk, and chickpeas. Season well with salt and pepper. Cook fc
about 5 minutes until the mixture begins to thicken.

Bean Burgers ★★★

erves 2-3   Preparation and cooking time: 30 mins

nese are fantastic. One of my sons - a confirmed carnivore who will hardly touch anything
~een - devoured these, and said they were delicious! I think this is a good recommendation.
you want to keep one of the burgers for the next day, don't fry it; but wrap it in cling film
nd keep it in the fridge.

x 750g pack of frozen broad beans
small onion, grated
slice bread, made into breadcrumbs
egg, beaten
bag crisps, crushed
il to fry

Toppings:
I onion, sliced
pickles
sauces

Allow the beans to defrost. Mash with a fork, or whizz a little with the blender. Don't make
nem too pulpy, leave a bit of texture.

Put the egg and breadcrumbs in a bowl, and allow the bread to soak up the egg. Mix well.
dd the beans.

Grate the onions and squeeze out most of the liquid. Add to the bean mixture and mix well.

Shape the mixture into 2-3 burgers. Put the crushed crisps on a plate, and roll the burgers
them. When they are coated in the crisps, heat oil in a frying pan, and cook the burgers for
bout 5 minutes each side. Take care that they do not burn. If they brown before the 5
ninutes just turn them. They will need a total of 10 minutes in order to be heated through.

While they are cooking slice the other onion (for the toppings) and fry in a saucepan until
aramelised (i.e. really brown). You will need to stir them frequently.

Slice the burger bun in half, horizontally. Put the burger inside, with the onions on top, and
ome sauce or pickle to finish. Enjoy!

Spicy Chick Peas ★★

Serves 2   Preparation time: 15 mins   Cooking time: 10 mins

Chickpeas are high in protein and inexpensive. This dish is ideal to heat up again the next day, but be careful not to overcook the spinach. Serve with jacket potatoes, or rice and yogurt.

I x 400g can chick peas, well rinsed
I tablespoon oil
½ red onion, chopped
2 tomatoes, chopped
⅔ mug water + I vegetable stock cube

handful of spinach
2 teaspoons curry paste
mug grated cheese
salt and pepper
yogurt to serve

1. Heat the oil in a saucepan and fry the onion until it becomes soft.
2. Add the tomatoes, curry paste, water, crumbled stock cube, and chick peas. Bring to the boil and then simmer for about 10 minutes.
3. Add the spinach and stir until it wilts; about 30 seconds.
4. Stir in the cheese and it will melt. Season with salt and pepper.
5. Serve with jacket potatoes and yogurt.

Bean Casserole ★

Serves 2   Preparation time: 10 mins   Cooking time: 15 mins

This casserole is simple to prepare. Eat it on it's own, or with baked potatoes or rice. You can vary the beans used, and add other vegetables if you wish. They will need to be quick-cook vegetables, such as mushrooms, or courgettes; not root vegetables.

1 x 400g tin cannellini beans
1 tablespoon olive oil, to fry
1 stick celery, chopped
1 clove garlic, chopped
3 small shallots (very small onions)
3 medium tomatoes, cut into chunks
½ mug water + 1 vegetable stock cube
1 dessertspoon tomato puree
salt and pepper

1. Heat the oil in a saucepan, and fry the onions, garlic, and celery for 3-4 minutes. Add the tomatoes, and cook for a further 3-4 minutes. Add the water and crumbled stock cube, and cook for another 2-3 minutes.
2. Rinse the beans well, and add, along with the tomato puree. Bring to the boil. Turn the heat down, and cook for 2-3 minutes to heat the beans through. Season well and serve.

Spanish Baked Eggs ★★

Serves 2   Preparation time: 15 mins   Cooking time: 15 mins

This is a variation on a Spanish dish. Eggs are baked in the oven on top of a tomato and olive mixture. Best cooked for 2 and shared, since the eggs won't reheat too well. You can eat it cold with some salad. You could eat it with some vegetarian sausages if you like.

2 large potatoes, washed and diced
1 tablespoon olive oil
1 small onion, cut into wedges
1 clove garlic, chopped
½ x 400g can chopped tomatoes
½ green pepper, chopped

½ teaspoon paprika
18 pitted black olives
4 eggs
1 teaspoon chives
salt and pepper

1. Preheat the oven to 200°C/gas mark 7.
2. Cook the diced potatoes in boiling water for about 10 minutes. Drain.
3. Heat the oil in a frying pan, and cook the onion, garlic, and peppers for 3-4 minutes. Add the tomatoes, paprika, chives, and olives. Cook for 5 minutes. Add the potatoes and mix well.
4. Place in a greased casserole dish. Make 4 hollows in the mixture, and break an egg into each. Season with salt and pepper.
5. Bake in the oven for 15 minutes, or until the eggs are cooked.

Eggs and Cheese

Cheese loaf ★ ★ ★

Makes 1 loaf   Preparation time: 15 mins   Cooking time: 30 mins

You could spread this with butter and eat with more cheese and pickles. You could also cook the mixture more like scones; i.e. tip it out onto a board and flatten to about 2", then cut up into about 12 and bake. If you do this you would need to reduce the cooking time to 15-20 minutes. You could then put half the cooked scones in the freezer and use at a later date.

1 handful of spinach
1" cube butter
1 leek, chopped
1½ mugs self raising flour
¾ mug parmesan cheese

salt and pepper
1 teaspoon basil
1 mug grated cheddar cheese
¾ mug milk

1. Preheat the oven to 170°C/gas mark 5.
2. Fry the leeks in a frying pan in the butter. When they are soft add the spinach, and cook for about 30 seconds until it wilts.
3. In a bowl, mix the flour, salt and pepper, cheeses, and basil. Add the leeks and spinach from the frying pan. Mix.
4. Gradually add milk, until it forms a ball in the bowl. You do not necessarily need to use all the milk. It should not be too sticky.
5. Grease a loaf tin, and then press the mixture evenly into it. Bake in the oven for 30-35 minutes. Once cooked, leave to cool and then slice.

Goat's Cheese Tart ★ ★ ★

Serves 2   Preparation time: 15 mins   Cooking time: 25 mins

You can use the base of this tart almost like a pizza. Add tomato sauce, plus some vegetables and cheese, and invent your own pizzas. The mini pizzas in nosh4students are also a good idea.

Base

oil to fry
½ onion, finely chopped
1 egg, beaten
1 mug self raising flour
⅛ x 250g block butter

Topping

125g packet of soft goat's cheese
15-18 black olives
8 cherry tomatoes
olive oil, to drizzle over the top

1. Fry the onion in the oil until it begins to brown. Set aside.
2. Preheat the oven to 180°C/gas mark 6.
3. Put the flour in a bowl and rub in the butter. Add the onions and the beaten egg. If the mixture is still dry, add a little more milk.
4. Tip out on to a surface and squash together. Place on a greased baking tray, and squash out gently with your fingers to make a round. It should be about ½" thick.
5. Cut the tomatoes in half, and spread over the top with the olives and the crumbled cheese. Drizzle oil over the top.
6. Bake in the oven for 25 minutes. Serve with salad, and sprinkle some French dressing over the tart.

Cheese Rissoles ★ ★

Serves 2   Preparation time: 15 mins

These rissoles go well with many of the salads you will find in this book. You can eat one and save the other for the next day, or the day after. You can eat them with salad and/ or baked potatoes.

½ x 100g packet of pine nuts, or cashews
3 heaped tablespoons cottage cheese
I teaspoon chives
2 spring onions, chopped
½ x 150g pack of quality flavoured crisps
salt and pepper

1. Either chop the nuts quite small, or whizz them with the blender; but don't make them too fine.
2. Crush the crisps whilst in the bag. Use the bottom of a bottle or jar. Put the crisps in a small bowl.
3. Mix together the nuts, cottage cheese, chives, and onions. Season with salt and pepper. Shape the mixture into 2 patties (see photo). Roll them in the crushed crisps to coat them. Leave them in the fridge for about half an hour, and they will become more solid.
4. Serve them with salad and salad dressing (pages 30-39).

Eggs and Cheese

Serves 2   Preparation and cooking time: 25-30 mins

This recipe is quite spicy. You can vary the type and amount of curry paste you use. If you wish, you can stir the yogurt into the curry at the end of the cooking time; this will make it milder.

I tablespoon oil, to fry
I medium onion, sliced
I tablespoon curry paste
I x 230g can of chopped tomatoes

4 eggs
½ mug frozen peas
2 tablespoon Greek yogurt
rice and mango chutney to serve

1. Heat the oil in the frying pan, add the onion, and cook for 5 minutes until it begins to go brown. Stir frequently. Add the tomatoes, peas, and curry paste. Bring to the boil, then simmer for 20 minutes.
2. Meanwhile, put the eggs on to boil for 8 minutes. When cooked, run cold water over them, and then peel. Cut each egg in half.
3. Gently stir them into the curry. Serve with yogurt, rice, and mango chutney.

No Pastry Quiche ★★

Serves 2   Preparation time: 20 mins   Cooking time: 25 mins

Here's a quiche without the bother of making pastry: much better for you, and very simple. You can add other vegetables to the basic recipe: broccoli, squash, etc.; but they need to be pre-cooked. If you cook this quantity, you can eat the other half the next day, cold.

1 tablespoon oil, to fry
1 pepper, cut into chunks
4 cherry tomatoes, cut in half
1 courgette, cut into chunks
1 red onion, cut into wedges

3 eggs, beaten
⅓ mug milk
1 tablespoon red pesto
salt and pepper

1. Preheat the oven to 180°C/gas mark 6.
2. Fry the onion, pepper, and courgette in the oil for 5 minutes, until they begin to brown. Transfer to a greased casserole dish. Add the tomatoes.
3. Beat the eggs in a bowl, and add the milk and pesto. Mix well. Season, and pour over the vegetables. Cook in the oven for 20-25 minutes, until the top begins to brown.
4. Serve either hot or cold, with salad or baked potatoes.

Savoury Cheesecake ★★★★

Serves 2-3   Preparation time: 20 mins   Cooking time: 20-25 mins

As the title suggests this is a kind of cheesecake. It is quite rich, and therefore best served with a refreshing salad. Again, you could vary the vegetables which are included. Use mainly those you can grate: celeriac, sweet potato, butternut squash, etc.

2 large potatoes, cut into ¼" slices
1 tablespoon oil to fry
1 leek, chopped
1 small courgette, grated
1 small carrot, grated
1 pepper, diced

1 teaspoon chives
300g pack cream cheese
½ mug grated cheddar cheese
2 eggs
salt and pepper

1. Preheat the oven to 170°C/gas mark 5. Grease a casserole dish.
2. Fry the sliced potatoes in a frying pan, until they are browned. Drain off the oil and put on a plate.
3. If necessary, add more oil to the pan; and fry the leek, pepper, courgette, and carrot.
4. Beat the eggs in a bowl, and add the cheeses. Mix well. Add the chives, fried courgette, carrot, pepper, and leek to the bowl. Season well and mix together.
5. Place the fried potatoes on the bottom of a casserole dish to form a base. Pour the cheese and vegetable mixture over the top.
6. Bake in the oven for 20-25 minutes until the cheese and egg mixture is set, but not too hard! It will brown a little. Serve with fresh salad.

Eggs and Cheese

Cheese and Potato Bake ★ ★

Serves 2   Preparation time: 15 mins   Cooking time: 30 mins

You can vary the combination of vegetables and cheeses, according to what you have in the fridge. This recipe uses frozen vegetables; although, they are not quite as good as when fresh. It is a good idea to keep a pack of frozen, mixed vegetables in your freezer drawer.

2 large potatoes, cut into ¼" slices   1 small courgette, cut into chunks (see photo)
1 red onion, sliced   1 tomato, cut into wedges
1 clove garlic, chopped   ½ x 225g pack of tofu, cut into chunks OR
1 x quick cheese sauce (page 20)   ½ x 200g pack of feta cheese, cut into cubes
1 mug mixed, frozen vegetables   ½ mug grated cheddar cheese

1. Boil the potatoes for 10 minutes. They do not need to be completely cooked because they will cook in the oven.
2. While they are cooking, make the cheese sauce (page 20).
3. Preheat the oven to 180°C/gas mark 6.
4. Fry the onions, garlic, and courgettes in a frying pan for 4-5 minutes, until they begin to brown. Stir frequently. Mix into the cheese sauce along with the other vegetables, and the tofu or feta cheese. Season well.
5. Pour this mix into a greased casserole dish. Arrange the sliced potatoes over the top. Sprinkle with grated cheese. Bake in the oven for 25-30 minutes, until the cheese has browned.

Mexican Eggs ★★

Serves 1   Preparation time: 15 mins

This dish makes a spicy breakfast alternative, or an interesting snack.

1 corn tortilla Oil for frying 3 small pieces of jalapeno chilli small clove of garlic, chopped 2 spring onions, chopped 1 tomato, cut into chunks 3 eggs, beaten 1 teaspoon chives salt and pepper	1. Cut the tortilla into strips, and fry in oil until golden brown. Set aside. 2. In the same frying pan, after tipping out most of the oil, fry the onions, garlic, and chopped chillies for 1 minute. Add the tomatoes and fry for another minute. 3. Add the beaten eggs and chives, and stir. Do not overcook the eggs; they need to be quite soft. Season with salt and pepper. 4. Put the tortilla strips on the plate and pour the egg mixture on top.

Courgette Torte ★ ★

Serves 2   Preparation time: 15 mins   Cooking time: 25 mins

This is a torte with a spicy twist. Eat it on its own, with green salad, or one of the other salads in this book. Here it is served only with fresh tomatoes.

2 medium courgettes, sliced
1 tablespoon oil
1 small onion, chopped
1 fresh green chilli, chopped

2 eggs
½ teaspoon paprika
½ mug grated cheddar cheese

1. Preheat the oven to 170°C/gas mark 5. Grease a casserole dish.
2. Fry the courgettes in a frying pan. When one side has browned, turn over and brown the other side. Transfer to a casserole dish.
3. Fry the onion and the chilli, until they begin to brown. Add to the courgettes in the casserole dish.
4. Beat the eggs, then add the paprika to them. Pour the egg mixture over the courgettes. Sprinkle the cheese over the top. Bake in the oven for 25-30 minutes until the cheese has browned and the eggs are set.

Serves 1   Preparation time: average 15 mins

Stir-fry is something of a staple dish for vegetarian students. Here is a basic method, plus a few variations for you to work on. If you want to use root vegetables (potatoes, carrots, parsnips, swedes, etc.) , you will need to pre-cook them (page 13) . Pictured below is ginger and corn stir fry.

6 pieces baby sweet-corn
1 tablespoon oil to fry
1 clove garlic, chopped
1 teaspoon freshly grated ginger
½ red pepper, sliced
6 sugar snaps
2 spring onions, chopped
½ mug water with 1 vegetable stock cube, crumbled
2 tablespoons soy sauce
½ x 200g pack of ready-to-use noodles
2" piece of courgette, sliced
3 small florets of broccoli
salt and pepper

1. Heat the oil in a wok. If you do not have one, a frying pan is fine. Fry the garlic, ginger, and onion for 1-2 minutes, then add the rest of the ingredients apart from the noodles. Keep the heat high, and cook for 4-5 minutes until the vegetables are cooked, and almost all of the liquid has reduced.
2. Stir in the noodles. Heat for 1 minute.
3. Season well with salt and pepper and eat straight away.

Stir-frying is easy. To avoid overcooked vegetables, use only a small amount of water, stock, or sauce. Cut the vegetables up quite small; this looks better and cooks quicker. Cook the onions and garlic first, then add the other ingredients. Soy sauce, chilli sauce, hoisin sauce, etc., are great to use. Keep a few of these sauces in your store cupboard

Cashews and vegetables - Firm tofu (¼ pack), 1 teaspoon hoisin sauce, 1 tablespoon cashews, half a chopped pepper, 1 clove garlic, chopped, 2 chopped spring onions, 6-8 sugar snaps, 1 vegetable stock cube (crumbled), and a handful of bean sprouts.

Creamy vegetables - Oil to fry; 1 small, chopped onion; 1 finely chopped carrot; 2 thin slices of aubergine; 2 sliced mushrooms; half a green pepper, or red pepper, sliced or chopped; 1 vegetable stock cube, crumbled; and add 2 tablespoons of double cream as the cooking sauce.

Spinach - 2 sliced spring onions; 1 finely chopped clove garlic; half a pepper, thinly sliced; 1 teaspoon soy sauce; 1 teaspoon honey; and add a handful of spinach with 2 tablespoons of nuts at the end of the cooking time.

Tomato with vegetables - Half an onion, chopped finely; 1 clove garlic, finely chopped; 1 courgette, sliced; half a pepper, sliced; 2 slices of aubergine; 2 mushrooms, sliced; fry all these first, then add half a tin of chopped tomatoes + 1 teaspoon of HP sauce. Cook for 3-4 minutes.

Bean sprouts and vegetables - 2 spring onions, chopped; 1 clove garlic, chopped; 1 sliced pepper; 1 sliced courgette; 2 sliced mushrooms; 6 sugar snaps; 1 teaspoon soy sauce; 1 teaspoon sugar; then add a handful of bean sprouts and a tablespoon pine nuts at the end.

Tofu and vegetables - 1 carrot, thinly sliced; a handful of green beans; 1 teaspoon, grated, fresh ginger; 1 clove garlic, chopped; 3 or 4 florets of cauliflower. Cook all these first in a little oil, add 1 teaspoon hoisin sauce, and then add about a quarter of a Chinese cabbage, chopped; 1 teaspoon honey. Add the tofu with a squeeze of lemon juice at the end.

Other things to add to stir fry -
egg noodles: a handful per person
rice noodles: a handful per person
rice: half a mug of cooked rice per person

Omelette strips. To make these: beat an egg, and before you start cooking the vegetables, put a little oil in the pan, pour in the egg and spread it around the pan, just like a pancake. Cook until it is brown on one side, then turn it over. When cooked take out of the pan and cut into strips. Add to the stir fry at the end. Use 1 egg per person.

Fried tortilla wraps: fry and cut into strips and add at the end to keep them crisp. Use one tortilla per person.

Other things to use as sauces -

coconut milk mixed with a teaspoon of curry paste
chilli sauce
tomato sauce
vegetable stock

Fajitas ★★

Serves 1   Preparation time: 15 mins

This is a recipe for a basic fajita. On the opposite page are some ideas for variations.
Fajitas have become so cosmopolitan the fillings are no longer restricted to Mexican flavours.
Serve them with salsa (page 88).

2 tortilla wraps
½ an onion, sliced
2 mushrooms, sliced
1 small clove of garlic, chopped
½ red or green pepper, sliced
1 dessertspoon tomato puree, mixed with a little water
oil to fry

1. Heat the oil in a frying pan. Fry the onion and the garlic for 1 minute; add the peppers and
mushrooms, and cook for 3-4 minutes until they are tender.
2. Add the tomato puree and water. Stir well, and cook for another 2-3 minutes to allow the
flavours to mix.
3. Warm the tortillas under the grill for about 1 minute. Put half the mixture onto each of the
tortilla wraps, roll them up, and eat!

Different vegetables, etc.

courgettes, cut into thin strips
mange tout or sugar snaps, cut into 2
peas
sweetcorn or baby corn cobs
beans sprouts
celery
butternut squash, pre-cook for 10 minutes
before adding at the end of stage 1.
beans: cannelini, pinto, haricot, etc.
spinach
roasted peppers; you can buy them in jars or
roast them yourself (page 13).
tomatoes
pine nuts

Cheeses - add after cooking

feta, crumbled
goat's cheese
grated cheddar
quick cheese sauce to pour over
(page 20).
tofu, cut into cubes and add at
the end of the cooking time.

Sauces

1 teaspoon chilli sauce
1 teaspoon HP sauce
1 dessertspoon tomato sauce
1 teaspoon hoisin sauce
1 tablespoon pesto + 1 teaspoon
water, or 1 tablespoon cream
½ teaspoon curry paste +
1 teaspoon water

Serve with -

salsa (page 88)
yogurt
different sauces (pages 20 & 21)

Big Wraps

These are similar to fajitas but usually too large for you to pick them up in your hands and eat them. Cook some rice, or use leftover rice. If you add pilau rice flavouring whilst cooking, it tastes better. Cut up the vegetables (whichever you choose) into small pieces. Make the fillings as usual, and then add the rice at the end. Fill the warmed wrap, sprinkle grated cheese over, and fold the wrap up. Serve with salsa and yogurt.

Roasted vegetables are great in a big wrap. Use the same quantities as for the pasta with roasted vegetables (page 47), but mix with rice instead of the pasta. Place in the wrap, and sprinkle with some grated cheddar.

You can also add ½ a tin of chopped tomatoes + 1 teaspoon of chilli sauce or 1 teaspoon tomato puree with the rice.

Salsa

Salsa is very easy to make. You can buy salsa in jars from the supermarket, but they will not taste as good as these. If you are having a party, these will work out much cheaper than the bought variety. Salsa is good with tortilla chips, quesidillas, and big wraps.

Avocado Salsa

1 medium avocado, peeled and chopped into small pieces.
1 medium onion, finely chopped
2 medium tomatoes, chopped into small pieces
½ teaspoon chilli powder
¼ teaspoon paprika
½ teaspoon sugar
1 teaspoon lemon juice (this stops the avocado from discolouring).
salt and pepper

Prepare all the ingredients and mix together.

Front - avocado salsa, back - tomato and onion

Tomato and onion salsa

4 tomatoes, cut into small pieces
1 green chilli pepper
½ onion, chopped finely
1 teaspoon sugar
1 teaspoon lemon juice
salt and pepper

Prepare ingredients and mix together.

If you like your salsa really hot, then adjust the amount of chilli powder or chilli flakes. Fresh chillies always make a better flavour, but powder and flakes are fine to use. If you use fresh chillies, do be careful to wash your hands carefully after chopping them, and don't touch around your eyes!

Dipping salsa

1 teaspoon oil to fry
1 x 400g tin of chopped tomatoes
1 onion, finely chopped
3 cloves garlic, finely chopped
1 teaspoon sugar
½ tablespoon tomato puree
½ teaspoon paprika
1 teaspoon chilli flakes
2 teaspoon freeze dried chives.

1. Fry the onions and garlic in a pan until they begin to brown.
2. Add the tin of tomatoes, bring to the boil then add the tomato puree, chilli, paprika, and sugar. Simmer for 3 - 4 minutes.

Dipping salsa

Vegetable

Koftas ★ ★ ★ ★

Serves 3-4   Preparation time: 30 mins   Cooking time: 15 - 20 mins

These have 4 stars because they are fiddly and take some time, not because they are particularly difficult. My family (who are not vegetarians) devoured these as soon as the photograph was taken. The yogurt dressing really makes the dish, so don't miss out on it.

1 tablespoon oil to fry
½ onion, finely chopped
1 carrot, finely chopped
1 celery stick, finely chopped
1 clove garlic, finely chopped
1 chilli, deseeded and chopped
2 teaspoons curry paste
⅔ mug red lentils
1 tablespoon tomato puree
1½ mugs water
1 vegetable stock cube
1 mug fresh breadcrumbs
⅓ mug cashews
1 teaspoon coriander or oregano
1 small egg, beaten
salt and pepper

Yogurt dip

3 tablespoons natural yogurt
1 tablespoon mango chutney
1 teaspoon coriander or oregano

1. Heat the oil in a saucepan. Fry the onions, garlic, carrot, celery, and chilli for 2-3 minutes, until the onions start to soften.
2. Add the water, crumbled stock cube, curry paste, lentils, and tomato puree. Bring to the boil. Turn down to simmer, with the lid on, for 20 minutes. Check every now and then to see that it has not boiled dry, and to stir. If, after the 20 minutes, it is still very wet, cook for a further 5 minutes with the lid off. The mixture should be like a paste.
3. Chop or whizz the cashew nuts, but not too fine. Crumble the breadcrumbs (you can even give them a bit of a whizz with the blender). Add the bread, egg, coriander, nuts, and seasoning to the mixture in the pan. Stir well. Leave to cool for about half an hour.
4. Preheat the oven to 160°C/gas mark 4.
5. Grease a baking tray. Roll the mixture into balls (see photo). It should make about 20. Put them on a baking tray, and cook in the oven for 15-20 minutes, until they are brown.
6. Mix the dip ingredients together, and serve with the hot Koftas.

Hot Pot ★

Serves 2-3   Preparation time: 10 mins   Cooking time: 20 mins

This is a good basic recipe. You can add and subtract vegetables as you have them to hand.
You can also add different flavourings into the mix; chilli, curry paste, mustard, etc. You need
to have a good variety within the pot for it to taste good. Serve with crusty bread or baked
potatoes. This dish will reheat well the next day.

1 small onion	2 stick celery
1 carrot	1 x 400g tin pinto beans
1 parsnip	1 mug water + 1 vegetable stock cube, crumbled
¼ swede	1 teaspoon marmite or yeast extract
¼ celeriac	salt and pepper

1. Chop all the vegetables fairly small (see photo). Heat some oil in a saucepan, and fry them
until they begin to brown a little.
2. Add the rest of the ingredients. Bring to the boil, and then turn down to simmer for 20
minutes. Check to see that the vegetables are all cooked. Do not overcook them. Check the
seasoning and add more salt and pepper if necessary.

Shepherds Pie ★ ★

Serves 2   Preparation time: 15 mins   Cooking time: 25 minutes

This is a classic, but it does not include the bother of mashed potatoes you would normally expect with shepherds pie, and also has a lovely tasty cheese topping. If you want to cook it with Quorn see instructions in nosh4students. This is a bean version. If you want to spice it up, just add 2 teaspoons of HP sauce to the bean mixture, before it goes in the dish.

½ mug black-eyed beans
1 tablespoon oil for frying
½ onion, chopped
1 small carrot, chopped
1 clove garlic, chopped
5 mushrooms, sliced
1 x 400g can chopped tomatoes
1 teaspoon basil
1 vegetable stock cube, crumbled
1 teaspoon sugar

Topping
2 large potatoes, diced
1" cube butter
½ mug grated cheddar cheese

1. Preheat the oven to 180°C/gas mark 6. Put the diced potatoes on to boil for 10 minutes.
2. If you are using dried beans you will need to soak them overnight. Rinse, and then cook in a pan of water, bring to the boil, and then turn down to simmer for 20 minutes. It is much easier to use canned beans. Use half a tin.
3. Heat the oil in a saucepan. Fry the onions, carrots, mushrooms, and garlic. Allow them to brown a little. Add the tomatoes, beans, sauce (if you are using it), stock cube, basil, and sugar. Cook for 10 minutes until the vegetables are tender.
4. By now the potatoes should be cooked. Drain them and return them back into the pan. Add the butter, and shake the pan with the lid on until the butter is mixed. The potatoes should go a bit raggy round the edges.
5. Put the bean mixture in a casserole dish, and top with the potatoes. Sprinkle the cheese on top, and bake in the oven for 25 minutes until the cheese has browned.

Aubergine Curry ★ ★

Serves 2   Preparation time: 15 mins   Cooking time: 15 mins

This is a version of Brinjal Mollee. Aubergines are an extremely popular vegetable in India and go well with this tangy curry.

1 aubergine, sliced
1 tablespoon vegetable oil
1 onion, sliced
1 clove garlic, chopped
1 teaspoon freshly grated ginger
1 tablespoon curry paste
⅔ mug water
½ mug coconut cream/milk

1. Heat the oil in a saucepan and fry the onions, garlic, and ginger. When the onions begin to brown, add the curry paste, coconut milk, and water. Bring to the boil, and then add the aubergines.
2. Simmer for 15 minutes until the aubergine is soft.
3. Serve with rice and yogurt.

You can add other vegetables to this recipe, just remember to allow enough simmering time for the vegetables to cook. Use the timings on page 13 as a guide.

Sweet Potato Patties ★ ★ ★

Serves 2   Preparation time: 15 mins   Cooking time: 25 mins

Sweet potatoes have a delightful gentle flavour, which works well with a yogurt dressing and a little salad, as pictured here.

2 medium sweet potatoes
1 leek, chopped
1 clove garlic, chopped
oil to fry
salt and pepper

1 teaspoon freshly grated ginger
2 tablespoons sweetcorn
1 tablespoon fromage frais
Yogurt dressing (page 31)

1. Preheat the oven to 180°C/gas mark 6.
2. Peel the potatoes and cut into chunks. Boil in water for 10 minutes until they are tender.
3. Fry the leeks, garlic, and ginger in a frying pan for 2-3 minutes. Drain and add the sweetcorn. Take off the heat.
4. When the potatoes are cooked, mash them with a fork. Mix in with the rest of the ingredients and season with salt and pepper.
5. Grease a baking tray and spoon the mixture into 4 or 5 piles. Brush the top with a little oil. Cook in the oven for 25 minutes until they are a little brown on the top.
6. Serve with the yogurt dressing and some salad.

Potato Pan Cake ★ ★ ★

Serves 2   Preparation and cooking time: 25 mins

This is an appetising, complete meal to make in one pan. You can use either tofu, or fet
cheese. You can also vary the vegetables if you wish; for example, sugar snaps, swee
potatoes, parsnips, and so on.

2 medium potatoes, diced
I small carrot, chopped
a few florets of broccoli
I tablespoon oil to fry
I small onion, chopped

I clove garlic, chopped
½ x 200 g pack of feta cheese or ½ x 390g pack tofu
2 tomatoes, cut into chunks
I mug grated cheddar cheese
salt and pepper

1. Cook the potatoes and the carrots in boiling water for about 5 minutes, then add the
broccoli. Cook for a further 5 minutes until everything is tender.
2. Turn the grill on to heat up.
3. Fry the onions, garlic, and tomatoes in a frying pan, allow them to brown a little. Add the
drained potatoes, broccoli, and carrots. Fry together for 2-3 minutes. Stir in the tofu or the
feta cheese, and season.
4. Sprinkle over the grated cheese, and put under the hot grill until the cheese browns. B
careful not to push the pan in too far, or the handle will burn. Serve immediately.

Potato Cakes ★ ★

Serves 2   Preparation and cooking time: 25 mins

You can make these potato cakes with or without the spice, depending on your taste, just leave out the chillies. Serve with baked beans, spicy chickpeas (page 72), or salsa.

2 large potatoes, diced
½ mug grated cheddar cheese
4 or 5 pieces of pickled jalepeno chillies, chopped
½ beaten egg
salt and pepper

2 teaspoon chopped chives
oil to fry
salsa (page 88)

1. Boil the potatoes for about 10-15 minutes until they are cooked. Mash lightly with a fork.
2. Add the chillies, cheese, chives, salt and pepper, and just enough egg to make everything stick together. If you add too much egg it will be difficult to fry. Form the mixture into 4 potato cakes.
3. Heat some oil in a frying pan. Fry the potato cakes on each side for about 4-5 minutes until they are browned.

Roast Wedges ★★

Serves 2   Preparation time: 10 mins   Cooking time: 15-20 mins

This dish of oven-baked vegetables makes a good accompaniment to bean burgers, or vegetarian sausages, but can make a meal in itself. You can vary the type of cheese, try some mozzarella, for instance.

1 large potato
2 tomatoes, cut into wedges
¼ mug water + 1 vegetable stock cube
1 tablespoon tomato puree
salt and pepper

2 mushrooms, sliced
½ yellow or red pepper, sliced
1 teaspoon chives
½ mug grated cheese

1. Preheat the oven to 170⁰C/gas mark 5.
2. Cut the potato into wedges. Boil for 10-15 minutes until cooked. Don't overcook or they will fall apart. Drain the potatoes and return to the pan. Add the peppers, mushrooms, and tomatoes.
3. Mix the tomato puree, chives, water, and crumbled stock cube together in a mug or small bowl. Pour over the vegetables in the pan, and mix.
4. Pour into a greased casserole dish and top with grated cheese.
5. Cook for 15-20 minutes until the cheese is browned.

Corn Cakes & Ratatouille ✱✱✱

Serves 2   Preparation and cooking time: 25 mins

These are best eaten straight away. You can keep the batter for making the corncakes in the fridge for the next day; but no longer. Ratatouille is a versatile dish, and goes well with bean burgers, vegetarian sausages, or any of the patty recipes in this book.

Ratatouille

1 tablespoon olive oil
1 onion, chopped
1 small clove garlic, chopped
1 baby aubergine, sliced
1 small courgette, sliced
1 red or green pepper, sliced
1 large mushroom, sliced
1 x 400g tin chopped tomatoes
salt and pepper

Corn cakes

⅔ mug self raising flour
1 x 130g can of sweetcorn, drained
1 egg
⅓ cup milk
oil to fry

To make the ratatouille: heat the oil in a saucepan. Add the onions and garlic, and cook for 3-4 minutes until the onions begin to brown. Add the other vegetables, one type at a time, and allow them to fry a little. When you have added them all, and they are beginning to cook, add the tomatoes. Season. Bring to the boil, and then turn down to simmer for 10 minutes.

While the ratatouille is cooking make the corn cakes. Put the flour in a bowl. (You can use half ordinary flour and half buckwheat flour if you wish.) Make a well in the centre, and add the egg and some of the milk. Beat with a wooden spoon. Add enough milk to make a thick, creamy consistency. Add the drained corn; this will make the batter thinner.

Heat the oil in a frying pan. Drop 3 or 4 separate heaped tablespoons of the batter mixture into the pan. Allow them to cook, and become solid and browned underneath. Turn them over, and allow them to brown on the other side. They should be cooked in the middle. If not, turn down the heat and cook for a little longer. Serve together with the ratatouille.

Squash and Apple Curry ⭐

Serves 2   Preparation time: 10 mins   Cooking time: 15-20 mins

This a yummy, sweet, mild curry. Serve with yogurt, naan bread, and rice.

I dessertspoon oil to fry
I small onion, chopped
½ butternut squash
2 large potatoes, diced
I eating apple, cored, and chopped into chunks

I teaspoon curry paste
I mug water
I vegetable stock cube
I tablespoon raisins
naan bread, rice, and yogurt to serve

1. Heat the oil in a saucepan. Add the onions, potatoes, and squash, and fry for 5 minutes un
they begin to brown.
2. Add the apple, water, crumbled stock cube, raisins and curry paste. Bring to the boil. Tu
down the heat, put the lid on the pan, and simmer for 15-20 minutes, until the vegetables a
cooked.
3. Serve with rice, naan bread, and yogurt.

Savoury Pancakes ★ ★

avoury pancakes are made in exactly the same way as sweet ones. Add savoury fillings, and
ey can turn from fun food to a serious meal.

ancakes

eggs

tablespoons plain flour (you can use
ne half bulgar wheat flour and one
alf plain flour).

ilk

rex or white Flora to fry (you can use
il but a lard type is best).

Suggested fillings

You can use any of the fillings for fajitas (page
86 & 87) or the 'big wrap' fillings.

Use some of the different sauces (page 20 &
21). Here, quick cheese sauce has been used.

   Beat the eggs and flour together in a bowl or jug. Gradually add the milk whilst mixing,
aking sure there are no lumps. The mixture should be as thin as single cream; quite thin,
ut not as thin as milk.

   Heat about ½" cube of lard in a frying pan. When the fat begins to smoke a little, pour
pproximately 2 tablespoons of the mixture into the pan. Tip the pan around so that the
ixture spreads over the surface of the pan. Let the mixture cook for about I minute.

   Gently lift the edge of the pancake to see if it is browned. Once browned, turn the pancake
th a slotted turner, or toss; and then cook the other side. Serving suggestions above.

Veggie Bake ★★

Serves 2   Preparation time: 20 mins   Cooking time: 30 mins

Veggie bake is another easy, basic recipe, which can be varied by using different vegetable
and also different sauces. Here I have suggested a ready-made cook-in-sauce. If you lo
carefully at the ingredients' labels, you will find a number that qualify as vegetarian. Some
them are 'creamy' ones, and others are tomato based. Alternatively, you can use the toma
sauce or quick cheese sauce recipes on page 20 & 21. Always put the grated cheese on th
top to give a tasty crunch.

Dolmio Creamy Mushroom Sauce used above

1 carrot, diced	3-4 cherry tomatoes
1 potato, diced	4-5 spring onions or 1 small onion, chopped
1 piece of butternut squash, cut into	1 teaspoon chives
chunks	½ mug grated cheese
1 courgette, sliced	1 jar cook-in-sauce

1. Boil the carrots, potatoes, squash, and any other root vegetables you are using for
minutes.
2. Preheat the oven to 180°C/gas mark 6.
3. Fry the onions and courgettes (also mushrooms if you are using them). Once they beg
to brown, take off the heat.
4. Drain the root vegetables, and return them to the pan. Add the onions and courgette
together with the tomatoes, chives, and cook-in-sauce. Mix together, and then pour into
greased casserole dish. Top with grated cheese. Bake in the oven for 25-30 minutes until th
cheese is browned.

Tofu Balls & Tomato Sauce ★★

Serves 2   Preparation time: 15 mins   Cooking time: 30 mins

When cooked these tofu balls have a delish, crunchy outside and a soft inside. The tomato sauce is essential. Serve with rice.

1 small onion, finely chopped
1 small garlic clove, finely chopped
½ x 375g pack tofu
¼ mug breadcrumbs
1 tablespoon flour
1 teaspoon soy sauce
1 teaspoon chives
1 teaspoon basil

Tomato sauce

1 tablespoon oil
1 medium onion, chopped
1 x 400g can chopped tomatoes
salt and pepper

1. Preheat the oven to 180°C/gas mark 6.
2. Put all the tofu balls' ingredients together in a bowl and mix well. Form into balls and place on a greased baking tray. Cook in the oven for 25-30 minutes, until they are browned.
3. While they are cooking, put the rice on to cook, and make the sauce.
4. Fry the onions in a saucepan, add the tomatoes, and cook for about 5 minutes. Season with salt and pepper. Whizz with the blender.

Baked Vegetable Patties ★ ★ ★

Serves 2   Preparation time: 15 mins   Cooking time: 25 mins

These are appetising, and baking in the oven gives a 'roasted' flavour. If you have a little cream handy, make the spicy sauce to go with them. If not, make one of the sauces on pages 20 & 21.

1 medium potato, diced
½ an onion, grated
1 small carrot, grated
1 courgette, grated
1 stick celery, finely chopped
1 vegetable stock cube
½ teaspoon oregano
¼ mug grated parmesan cheese
1 beaten egg
oil to fry

Chilli sauce

2 tablespoons cream
½ vegetable stock cube, crumbled
¼ teaspoon chilli flakes
½ teaspoon oregano.

1. Preheat the oven to 180°C/gas mark 6.
2. Boil the potatoes for about 10 minutes until they are soft. Drain well, and mash with a fork. Add the grated onion, carrot, courgette, cheese, oregano, and the celery. Crumble the stock cube over and mix. Add the egg a little at a time, taking care that the mixture does not get too soft. You will probably only need half the egg.
3. Grease a baking tray and pile the mixture into 3-4 piles. Shape into rounds. Cook in the oven for 25 minutes; the patties should go slightly brown.
4. To make the sauce, simply put all the ingredients in a pan and heat. Do not boil.

Mushroom Stroganoff

Serves 2   Preparation and cooking time: 15 mins

This is a classic vegetarian dish and scrumptious. Try this one if your cooking skills are not too well honed. You can eat half, then save the other half for the next day.

I small onion, chopped finely
2 celery sticks, sliced finely
12 medium mushrooms, sliced
I tablespoon oil to fry
I dessertspoon flour

I vegetable stock cube, dissolved in ½ mug water
I dessertspoon chives
2 tablespoons soured cream
salt and pepper

. Put the oil in the pan, and fry the onions and celery until they are transparent.
2. Add a little more oil to the pan, add the mushrooms, and cook for 2-3 minutes.
3. Add the flour to the pan. Mix together, and then add the crumbled stock cube and water.
Bring to the boil, then turn down the heat and simmer, uncovered, for 2-3 minutes.
4. Take off the heat, and add the soured cream and the chives. Season with salt and pepper.
Serve with rice. See page 11 for how to cook rice.

Spicy Chips ★★

Serves 2   Preparation time: 10 mins   Cooking time: 40 mins

This is how to make chips the safe way; without deep frying. Also they are slightly more healthy. If you don't want your chips spicy, don't add the curry paste to the oil.

2 large potatoes
1 large sweet potato
¼ mug oil
1 teaspoon curry paste

1. Preheat the oven to 180°C/gas mark 6.
2. Peel the sweet potato. You do not need to peel the ordinary potatoes, just wash them. Cut them all into chips.
3. Place the chips on a baking tray. Using a mug, mix the curry paste with the oil, and sprinkle over the chips. Toss the chips in the oil to make sure they are all covered. Spread them out on the tray.
4. Cook in the oven for 40 minutes. They should be nicely browned by this point.

Vegetables

Roast Veg with Tofu ★

Serves 1   Preparation time: 10 mins   Cooking time: 45 mins

Tofu is high in protein and contains calcium, iron, and Vitamins B1, B2 and B3. It is, however, fairly bland in taste and therefore needs to be eaten with other, more tasty foods.

½ x 350g block of tofu
½ onion cut into wedges
¼ butternut squash, cut into pieces
small sweet potato, or normal potato

1 small courgette
1 teaspoon rosemary (optional)
1 tablespoon oil
salt and pepper

1. Preheat the oven to 190°C/gas mark 7.
2. Cut the vegetables into chunks (see photo).
3. Cut the tofu up into chunks.
4. Place all the ingredients into a casserole dish, sprinkle olive oil over, and mix to cover all the ingredients in oil. Season with salt and pepper, and sprinkle with rosemary if you have some. Bake in the oven for 45 minutes until nicely browned.

Muffins ★★

Makes 12 +   Preparation time: 15 mins   Cooking time: 20 mins

Muffins are really quick and easy to make, and there are many variations. There are a few listed here, and a few more in the original nosh4students book. Try some.

picture shows summer fruits muffins

Basic recipe
3 mugs self raising flour
1 mug brown sugar (you can use white)
2 eggs, slightly beaten
1½ mugs milk
¾ mug vegetable oil

1. Preheat the oven to 180°C/gas mark 6.
2. Mix the dry ingredients together, then add the wet ones. Stir together. The mixture will be a bit lumpy but do not overmix.
3. If you have cake tins, use them and put paper cake cases in each hole. If you do not have cake tins, put double paper cake cases for each muffin on your baking tray. This will help the cases hold their shape. Spoon the mixture into each case.
4. Bake in the oven for 20 minutes. If you use the larger muffin cases you will need to bake them for 25 minutes. They should be a little brown and spring back when gently pressed.

Variations

Summers fruits

Just add ½ x 500g bag of frozen summer fruits, and bake as usual.

Apple

Add 2 cooking or eating apples, cored and chopped up, + 1 teaspoon cinnamon.

Dates

Add 1 mug chopped dates, 2 teaspoons ground ginger, ½ teaspoon cinnamon, and the grated rind of an orange.

Nuts

Add 1 mug chopped pecan nuts + 2 teaspoons instant coffee grains.

White chocolate and berry

Add 1 x 100g pack of white chocolate chips and ½ x 500g pack frozen fruits of the forest,

Apricot and marmalade

Replace ½ mug flour, with muesli. Add 100g ready-to-eat apricots, chopped; and the grated rind of 1 orange. When the mixture is in the cases, but before it goes into the oven, drop 1 teaspoon of marmalade into the centre of each muffin. Bake as usual.

Honey and Oats

Replace ½ mug of flour with ½ mug oats, and add ½ teaspoon cinnamon, ½ mug raisins, and 5 tablespoons of honey.

Banana and nut

Squash 2 large bananas and add when the mixture is wet, together with ½ mug chopped nuts.

Cranberry and poppy seed

Add 4 teaspoons poppy seeds to the dry ingredients and a 140g pack of cranberries to the wet ingredients.

Once you have the hang of these variations, you can experiment with your own varieties. Don't put anything too wet into the ingredients, and don't add more liquid. If you want to add something very wet then reduce the quantity of milk by a proportional amount.

Orange Chocolate Cake ★★★

Serves 12-16   Preparation time: 20 mins   Cooking time: 50-55 mins

You will need to buy a cake tin if you want to make this one. It would make a great birthday cake for someone. It is very easy to make and most of us like chocolate/ orange flavour.

3 oranges
3 eggs
1¼ mugs sugar
¾ mug sunflower oil
½ x 200g block dark chocolate

3 tablespoons cocoa
1½ mugs self raising flour

Topping

200g block dark chocolate
1 mug double cream

1. Preheat the oven to 160°C/gas mark 5. Grease a cake tin and put a circle of greaseproof paper in the bottom.
2. Break up the chocolate and melt, gently, in a saucepan. Once melted, take off the heat.
3. Grate the rind from one of the oranges. Place in a mixing bowl. Peel all 3 oranges and put the flesh in the bowl with the grated rind. Discard all the peel and pith. Whizz with the blender.
4. Beat the eggs, and add to the bowl with the oil and sugar. Beat well.
5. By now the chocolate should have cooled a little, so add to the bowl and mix well.
6. Stir in the flour and the cocoa. Mix well, but do not beat. The mixture will be very wet; do not worry! Pour the mixture into the cake tin, and bake in the oven for 50-55 minutes. The cake should spring back when gently pressed.
7. To make the topping - put the cream in a saucepan, and bring to the boil and immediately take off the heat. Break up the chocolate, add to the cream, and stir until it melts. Leave to cool and it will start to set. Once the cake has cooled and the topping has begun to set, spread it over the top. Serve on its own or with cream.

Dream Bars ★★

Makes 18-20   Preparation time: 15 mins

These are heavenly. They are easy to make because they do not need cooking. You can vary the actual nuts and the seeds you use, just keep to the same amounts.

I mug ready-to-eat dried apricots
3½ mugs rice krispies
¾ mug desiccated coconut
½ x 100g pack of almonds, roughly chopped

½ x 100g pack of sunflower or pumkin seeds
⅔ mug brown sugar
2 rounded tablespoons golden syrup
⅖ x 250g block butter

1. Chop the apricots with some scissors. Put them in a bowl with the coconut, nuts, and rice krispies. Mix together.
2. Put the butter, sugar, and syrup in a pan and melt. Simmer for 30 seconds. The sugar should all be dissolved, and the mixture will be like toffee. The sugar is very hot at this point, so take care.
3. Pour immediately into the dry ingredients in the bowl. Mix fairly quickly and thoroughly, making sure that there are no dry patches.
4. Turn out into a greased baking tray. Press down so that it sticks together and spreads out. Leave for about I hour to set and cool. Cut into pieces and eat.

Apple Cake ★★★

Makes 18 pieces   Preparation time: 20 mins   Cooking time: 40 mins

The mixture of fruits and nuts in this cake are scrumptious. If you want to keep it from your ravenous friends, you can freeze half of it for a later date.

3 eggs
⅘ x 250g block of butter, melted
2 mugs self raising flour
2 teaspoons cinnamon
¾ mug sugar

2 medium eating apples
¾ mug dates, cut into pieces
½ x 200g pack brazil nuts, roughly chopped
3 tablespoons apricot jam

1. Preheat the oven to 160°C/gas mark 4. Grease a baking tray, and put some greaseproof paper over the bottom.
2. Core the apples, and cut into fairly small chunks. Put them in a bowl with the sugar, cinnamon, flour, dates, and nuts.
3. Melt the butter on a low heat. When it has cooled a little, add the eggs and gently beat . Pour this into the dry ingredients in the bowl. The mixture is quite dry, so needs to be mixed well.
4. Press evenly into a baking tray to make it level. Bake in the oven for 45-50 minutes. When the cake comes out of the oven, heat the jam in a pan until it becomes liquid. Don't let it boil. Spread over the top of the warm cake. Leave to cool and cut into squares.

Cashew Nut Cookies ★ ★ ★

Makes 16   Preparation time: 20 mins   Cooking time: 15 mins

Yummy cookies for you to have a go at. These have creamed coconut in them and when combined with the cashew nuts are very moreish. Don't give up when looking for the creamed coconut in the supermarket; ask, or try looking around the curry paste section.

1 mug cashew nuts, toasted and roughly chopped
½ x 200g packet of creamed coconut, grated
1 mug self raising flour
⅗ x 250g block butter
⅔ mug brown sugar
1 dessertspoon ground ginger (optional)
1 egg

1. Preheat the oven to 180°C/gas mark 6.
2. Cream the butter and sugar in a bowl, and beat in the egg.
3. Add the rest of the ingredients and mix well.
4. Tip out onto a floured surface, and squash into a long sausage. The dough is quite sticky. Cut into 16, and make each shape into a round; but do not squash too flat.
5. Place on a greased baking tray (you can cook in batches it you only have one tray). Bake in the oven for 15 minutes. The cookies should go golden brown.

Cherry Cookies ★ ★ ★

Makes 18   Preparation time: 20 mins   Cooking time: 15 mins

You can store the raw mixture for these cookies in the fridge for about a week. This way you can bake fresh cookies throughout the week.

I x 250g block butter
⅔ mug sugar
I mug self raising flour

2 mugs oats
200g pack of glace cherries
2 tablespoons mixed fruit or raisins

1. Preheat the oven to 160°C/gas mark 4.
2. Cream the softened butter and sugar together in a bowl until they are light and fluffy. Use a wooden spoon; this may take quite a few minutes.
3. Stir in the whole cherries, flour, fruit, and oats. It seems at first as though it will not mix in but it does.
4. Tip the mixture out onto a floured surface and squeeze together. Divide into approx. 18 pieces and roll into balls. Grease a baking tray and squash the balls down; so they are just over 1" thick. They will spread a bit when you cook them, so place them apart. Cook in the oven for 15 minutes; they should go golden brown and they are yummy. Don't eat straight away as the cherries are very hot!

Truffles ★ ★ ★

Makes 24 pieces   Preparation time: 15 mins   Standing time: 1 hour

These are really good when you have a few friends around to watch a video. nosh4students has a recipe for nachos; also good for parties and video nights.

200g block of dark chocolate
teaspoons vanilla extract
x 250g block butter
mug icing sugar

¾ mug ground almonds
grated chocolate, drinking chocolate, or
icing sugar to roll the truffles in.

Melt the chocolate and the butter in a saucepan over a very low heat. Be careful not to let get too hot.

Stir in the icing sugar, vanilla extract, and the ground almonds. Leave to cool. Don't put in the fridge or it will go hard; just leave in a cool place.

Once it has firmed up a bit, then take about a dessertspoon at a time and roll into balls. Roll them in the grated chocolate, drinking chocolate, or icing sugar.

Cakes and Biscuits

Nutty Honey Cake ★ ★

Makes 12 slices   Preparation time: 15 mins   Cooking time: 1 hour

As cakes go, this is quite nutritious, and the honey and date flavours come through nicely. I will keep for a week or so if kept in a tin, or a sealed bag.

1⅓ mugs self raising flour
½ teaspoon cinnamon
⅗ x 250g block butter
¾ mug brown sugar (white is OK)
3 tablespoons honey

2 eggs
I large banana
½ mug stoned dates, chopped
50g pack of pecan nuts (other varieties are OK)

1. Preheat the oven to 140°C/ gas mark 3. Grease a loaf tin. If you have greaseproof paper, cut an oblong and place over the bottom of the tin.
2. Peel and mash the banana in a fairly large bowl.
3. Add the eggs and beat together. Add the honey, dates, sugar, and the nuts. Mix well.
4. Melt the butter over a low heat in a pan, and then stir into the mixture in the bowl.
5. Add the flour and the cinnamon to the bowl. Mix well but do not beat vigorously.
6. Cook in the oven for 1 hour. The cake should spring back when pressed gently on the top.

Nutty Cookies ★ ★ ★

Makes 18   Preparation time: 15 mins   Cooking and fridge time: 45 mins

These are delicious pine nut cookies. The preparation time is lengthy, due to the time in the fridge; but they are well worth a try.

½ mug pine nuts
½ x 250g block butter
⅔ mug sugar

1 egg
1⅔ mug self raising flour

1. Cream the butter and sugar together with a wooden spoon in a bowl. Add the egg and beat well.
2. Add the flour and the nuts, and mix well. It will be a little stiff. Keep a few nuts for stage 6.
3. Press into a sausage shape about 12" long and cover with cling film. Leave in the fridge for half an hour.
4. Preheat the oven to 160°C/gas mark 4.
5. Cut the sausage into 16 or 18 pieces and squash each cookie into a round. Squash down to about ½" thick.
6. Place them on a greased baking tray and put a couple of pine nuts on each one. Bake in the oven for 12-15 minutes. They should go golden brown.

Crunchies ★★

Makes 24   Preparation time: 15 mins   Cooking time: 10-12 mins

These biscuits are crunchy on the outside and a bit gooey on the inside. SCRUMPTIOUS.

1 mug rolled oats
1 mug desiccated coconut
1 mug self raising flour
½ mug sugar

⅔ x 250g block butter
1 tablespoon golden syrup
2 tablespoon water

1. Preheat the oven to 170°C/gas mark 5.
2. Put all the dry ingredients in a bowl.
3. Melt the butter in a pan on a low heat. Add the syrup and the water, and stir.
4. Pour into the dry ingredients, and mix well.
5. Grease a baking tray. Take about a tablespoon of the mixture at a time, squeeze into a ball, and place on the baking sheet. Place them a little apart since they will spread as they cook. Put about 8 on the tray. If you only have one tray, it is OK to leave the mixture standing while each batch is baking.
6. Bake for 10-12 minutes until golden brown.

Nut & Apricot Bars ★★

Makes 18   Preparation time: 15 mins   Cooking time: 35-40 mins

These bars are lovely and moist. The crunchy nuts, soft apricots and apple are delicious.

x 100g pack of toasted, flaked almonds
⅓ mug ready-to-eat apricots, chopped
¾ mug porridge oats
⅔ mug self raising flour
x 250ml jar of apple sauce

2 tablespoons sunflower oil
I egg, beaten
2 tablespoons apricot jam

Preheat the oven to 160°C/gas mark 4.
. Mix the dry ingredients and the apricots in a bowl.
. Mix the egg, oil, and apple sauce together in a bowl, or jug. Mix into the dry ingredients, until everything is evenly distributed.
. Pour into a greased baking tray and press flat. Bake in the oven for 35-40 minutes until golden brown on the top.
. When the cake comes out of the oven, allow to cool for 2-3 minutes. While the cake cools, heat up the jam in a pan until it becomes liquid. Spread the jam over the top of the cake, either with a brush or spoon. Once cool, cut into bars.

Nut and Chocolate Squares ★★

Makes 18   Preparation time: 15 mins   Cooking time: 20-25 mins

This is, basically, classy flapjack. The nuts could almost make you think it is good for you but the chocolate will convince you otherwise. Either way, it is very delicious.

2 mugs rolled oats
3 tablespoons desiccated coconut
⅗ x 250g block butter
5 tablespoons golden syrup

½ cup brown sugar
1½ x 100g packs pistachios or other nuts (brazils and pistachios in photo)
1 x 100g packet of chocolate chips

1. Preheat the oven to 160°C/gas mark 4.
2. Put the oats and coconut in a bowl.
3. Put the butter, sugar, and syrup in a pan, and heat gently until the sugar has melted. Stir into the oat mixture. Mix well.
4. Press into a greased baking tray. Press the nuts and the chocolate into the top.
5. Cook in the oven for 20-25 minutes until golden brown. Allow to cool in the tray and then cut into pieces.

Date & Fig Squares ★★

Makes 18   Preparation time: 15 mins   Cooking time: 20 mins

This is a great way to eat dates and figs. These squares have a sticky middle, and a contrasting crumbly outside.

1 x 375g pack of ready-to-eat stoned dates
1 x 375g pack of ready-to-eat figs
grated rind of ½ lemon
2¾ mugs self raising flour

1 mug oats
½ mug brown sugar
⅗ x 250g block butter
⅓ mug water

Preheat the oven to 180°C/gas mark 6.

Put the dates, figs, water, and lemon rind in a saucepan. Heat gently, do not boil, until the fruits soften a little.

Put the flour into a bowl. Chop the butter up into small pieces, and rub into the flour. Add the oats and the sugar, and mix. This is the crumble mixture.

Put half the crumble mixture in the bottom of a greased baking tray. Spread the fruit mixture evenly over the top. Sprinkle the rest of the dry ingredients over the top, and press down gently.

Bake in the oven for 20 minutes; the top should be lightly browned. Cut into squares when cool.

Baked Pears ★★

Serves 2   Preparation time: 10 mins   Cooking time: 25 mins

This is a good looking, impressive, but surprisingly easy dessert to make. You can serve this with double cream, creme frais, fromage frais, yogurt, ice cream, or custard, depending on the occasion!

2 ripe pears
1 tablespoon lemon juice
2 tablespoons brown sugar
½ teaspoon ground cinnamon
1" cube butter
1 tablespoon water
lemon rind to serve (optional)

Serving suggestions
2 tablespoons yogurt, double cream, fromage frais, creme frais, or 1 tin custard, or ice cream.

1. Preheat the oven to 180°C/gas mark 6.
2. Peel the pears, halve them, and take out the cores. Try to leave the pear halves intact. Place them on the bottom of a greased casserole dish. Brush with the lemon juice, this stops the pears from going brown.
3. Place the sugar, cinnamon, butter, and water in a saucepan, and bring to the boil. Turn down to a low heat, and cook until the sugar is dissolved. Pour over the pears in the casserole dish.
4. Bake for 20-25 minutes. Serve with any of the suggestions above.

Fruity Rice ★

Serves 2   Preparation time: 5 mins

You can make this with most fruits. Here, I have used fruits of the forest, since they are amongst the most convenient fruits. You can used tinned fruits, but frozen are more healthy because tinned fruits usually have a lot of sugar added. Fresh fruit is, of course, the best. Strawberries, blackberries, blackcurrants, blueberries, and raspberries will work very well.

x 425g tin rice pudding
x 500g pack of frozen fruits of the forest
teaspoon vanilla extract

Place the rice pudding in a bowl, and stir in the vanilla extract.
Once the fruit is defrosted, place about 1 tablespoon in the bottom of each dish. If you have glass dishes, great, otherwise use cereal bowls. Put half the rice in each bowl. Add more fruit the top. Serve. Dead easy!

Baked Egg Custard ★★

Serves 2-3   Preparation time: 10 mins   Cooking time: 1 hour

Baked egg custard is a bit old fashioned, but remains a good way to eat eggs and fruit. It is quick to make, and will keep in the fridge for a few days if you cover it with cling film.

4 eggs
2 mugs milk
3 tablespoons brown sugar
1 teaspoon vanilla extract
½ teaspoon grated orange rind
½ mug raisins

1. Preheat the oven to 160°C/gas mark 4.
2. Beat the eggs and add the milk, sugar, and vanilla extract.
3. Grease a casserole dish, and put the raisins and orange rind in the bottom. Pour the eggs and milk over the top.
4. Place the casserole dish in the oven, and bake for 1 hour, or until the egg is set. If you shake the dish a little the custard should still wobble a bit.

Bread and Butter Pud ★ ★

Serves 2-3   Preparation time: 10 mins   Cooking time: 20-25 mins

This is a good way to use up any leftover bread. You can use any type of bread. You can also add other things like chopped-up apricots, spoonfuls of marmalade, honey, and other dried fruits.

slices of bread
butter to spread
tablespoons sugar
tablespoons raisins

1 mug milk
3 eggs
¼ teaspoon cinnamon (optional)

Preheat the oven to 180°C/gas mark 6.
Spread the bread with butter, and cut into 4 triangular pieces. Arrange them in a casserole dish.
Sprinkle the sugar and the raisins around the bread.
Beat the eggs, and add the milk and cinnamon. Pour over the bread.
Cook in the oven for 20-25 minutes. The bread should be browned, and the eggs set.

Tiramisu ★ ★ ★

Serves 4-6   Preparation time: 20 mins   Stand time: 1 hour

This version is a bit of a cheat but still tastes fantastic.

2 x 250g pots of mascarpone cheese
½ x 175g pack sponge fingers
1 x 425g tin custard
2-3 tablespoons brandy or rum

2 tablespoons instant coffee
+ 2 tablespoons water
2 tablespoons icing sugar
cocoa powder to finish

1. Mix the coffee with the water and alcohol. Dip the sponge fingers in the liquid and use them to line the bottom of a bowl. If you do not have a glass bowl, a casserole dish will do.
2. Soften the mascarpone cheese with a spoon, and mix in the custard and sugar, until it smooth. Pile on top of the sponge fingers.
3. Leave to set for about 1 hour, and then sprinkle cocoa on the top (see photo).

fruit fool ★

Serves 2   Preparation time: 15 mins

This is a bit of a 'dinner party' one. Looks good, and tastes fantastic. You can use other fruits to vary this very easy recipe. Suggested fruits: fruits of the forest, raspberries, mangoes, peaches, blueberries, and blackberries. It works best with fresh fruit.

2 kiwi fruits
6 large strawberries
1 x 425g tin of custard
½ x 450g pot of Greek yogurt with honey, or any other flavoured yogurt
4 sponge fingers
2 tablespoons orange juice. You can vary this according to the fruits you use.

Break the sponge fingers in two. Divide them among the glasses. I have used big wine glasses here. If you don't have any, just use cereal bowls. Pour the orange juice over the sponges.

Peel the kiwi fruits, and slice thinly. Wash and slice the strawberries.

Arrange the fruits, custard, and yogurt in 'areas', not so much layers (see photo). Make it look as pretty as possible.

Apple Crumble ★★

Serves 2   Preparation time: 15 mins   Cooking time: 20-25 mins

Apple crumble is an old fashioned recipe, but very versatile. You can add many fruits; blackberries, rhubarb, plums, etc. Cook the fruit in the same way as the apples, taking care not to overcook them and turn them into pulp. You can also use pie fillings, available in supermarkets.

2 large cooking apples
½ mug water
½ mug brown sugar (white is OK)
I teaspoon mixed spice (optional)

Topping
I mug plain flour
¼ x 250g pack butter
½ mug sugar

1. Preheat the oven to 180°C/gas mark 6.
2. Peel the apples and remove the core. Cut into chunks, and place in a pan with ½ mug of water. Bring to the boil and allow to cook for 3-4 minutes. The apples will begin to go fluffy round the edges, and soften. When they do, add the sugar and the mixed spice. (If you add the sugar at the beginning, the apples will stay hard.) Stir in the sugar, and pour into the bottom of an ovenproof dish. A casserole dish will do. Set aside while you make the topping.
3. Put the flour and butter in a bowl. With your fingers and thumbs, rub the butter into the flour until it looks a bit like breadcrumbs. Add the sugar, and mix. Gently spoon on top of the apple mixture, and spread evenly. Press down with a fork.
4. Cook in the oven for 20-25 minutes. Serve warm with custard, ice cream, or cream.

Sweet Pancakes ★★

erves 6   Preparation and cooking time: 25 mins

ancakes are good fun when you have friends around. Just make sure others are helping in
ie cooking process. Tossing them is always fun; catching them not guaranteed!

ancakes

 eggs
 tablespoons plain flour
iilk (see below)
rex or white Flora to fry
'ou can use oil but a
ird type is best)

Serving suggestions

lemon juice and sugar, undiluted squashes
any kind of ice cream
maple syrup, golden syrup
fruit, such as strawberries, or fruits of the forest
jam, or ice cream sauces
tinned pie fillings (cherry is shown in the photo).

   Beat the eggs and flour together in a bowl or jug. Gradually add enough milk until the
iixture is as thin as single cream; quite thin, but not as thin as milk. Make sure there are no
imps.
. Heat about ½" cube of lard in a frying pan. When the fat begins to smoke a little, pour
pproximately 2 tablespoons of the mixture into the pan. Tip the pan around, so that the
iixture spreads over the surface of the pan. Let the mixture cook for about 1 minute.
. Gently lift the edge of the pancake to see if it is browned. Once browned, turn the
ancake with a slotted turner, or toss, and then cook the other side. Serving suggestions
bove.

Baked Apples ★

Serves 1   Preparation time: 10 mins   Cooking time: 25-30 mins

A very simple, nutritious dessert, looks fantastic when you get it out of the oven, tastes yummy too. Serve with a little cream, yogurt, creme frais, or custard.

1 large cooking apple
1 tablespoon brown sugar
2 tablespoons sultanas or raisins

a little butter
1 dessertspoon honey
1 tablespoon water

1. Preheat the oven to 180°C/gas mark 6.
2. Wash the apple, and cut out the core from the centre, leaving the apple whole. Score a horizontal line around the centre of the apple (see photo). This stops the skin from bursting.
3. Mix together the sugar and the fruit. Stuff it into the space where the core was. Place on an ovenproof dish; a casserole dish is fine. Place small pieces of butter around the top of the apple. Spoon the honey over the apple, and then the water. If you have spare fruit and sugar, sprinkle around the bottom of the apple, and it will turn into toffee as the apple cooks.
4. Bake in the oven for 25-30 minutes.

Berry Trifle ★ ★

serves 4-6   Preparation time: 20 mins

ere is a more alcoholic version of this in the original nosh4students. However, if you want to
dd something like liqueur, sherry, brandy, or the like; add it to the swiss roll before you put
e fruits in. This is not an every day dish, but one you can use when you have friends around
r a meal.

x 500g pack of frozen summer fruits, defrosted
chocolate swiss roll
x 425g can of custard
mug or ½ pint of double cream
rated chocolate for the topping

Cut about 6-8 slices of the swiss roll, and arrange them on the bottom of a dish; a
asserole dish will be fine.
Pour the fruit on top and distribute evenly. Allow the juices to seep into the swiss roll.
Pour the custard over the fruit.
Beat the cream until it is thick. Be careful not to beat it too much, or you will have made
ourself some butter! Carefully spread over the top.
Grate some chocolate, and sprinkle over the top.

shopping

Menu 1

Monday	Nutty Veg Crumble (p.64)
Tuesday	Eat rest of Veg Crumble
Wednesday	Veggie Bake (p.100)
Thursday	Eat rest of Veggie Bake
Friday	Potato Hash (p.68)
Saturday	Mango and Noodle Salad (p.37)
Sunday	Classic Nut Roast (p.59)

+ roast potatoes, parsnips, and onions
+ tomato sauce. Eat with friends

Check cupboards

oil
chives
garlic
tomato puree
stock cubes
marmite
mixed herbs
plain flour

Shopping

Small bag of potatoes
3 parsnips
small piece of swede
1 sweet potato
1 carrot
2 peppers
1 small red chilli
4 onions
2 mushrooms
1 bunch spring onions
1 lettuce
few tomatoes
half cucumber
1 small mango
fruit for snacks
1 small pack cherry tomatoes

dried fruit and nuts for snacks
bread
butter or spread
milk
6 eggs
large block cheese
peanut butter
1 tin coconut milk
1 jar cook-in-sauce
2 x 400g tins tomatoes
1 tin beans
200g pack ready-to-eat egg noodles
200g pack cashew nuts
200g pack pine nuts

This shopping list assumes that you will eat sandwiches, fruit, or jacket potatoes for lunch each day. You will need to cook 5 times in the week

shopping

Menu 2

Monday	Nut and courgette Slice (p.62) + baked potatoes and yogurt dressing
..esday	Eat rest of Nut Slice + salad
Wednesday	Leek Soup (p27)
Thursday	Eat rest of Leek Soup
Friday	Sweet & Spicy Pilau (p.56) + salad
Saturday	Bean Casserole (p.73)
Sunday	Vegetable Lasagna (p.41) share with friends

Check cupboards

tomato puree
oil
garlic
salad dressing
chilli powder
mango chutney

Shopping

1 small bag potatoes
1 carrot
2 leeks
1 mushroom
3 onions
2 courgettes
1 red pepper
1 celery
6 tomatoes
1 lettuce
half cucumber
spring onions
3 shallots (small onions)
fruit for snacks
butter or spread

dried fruit and nuts for snacks
bread
milk
6 eggs
large block cheese
1 small pot natural yogurt
1 small pot double cream
1 x 400g tin cannellini beans
2 x 400g tin chopped tomatoes
lasagna strips
small packet currants
small packet raisins
small packet ready to eat apricots
small packet pine nuts
200g pack cashew nuts

This shopping list assumes that you will eat sandwiches, fruit or jacket potatoes for lunch each day. You will need to cook 5 times in this week.

Menu 3

Monday	Beanburgers (p.71)
Tuesday	Eat rest Beanburgers + salad
Wednesday	Pasta and Broccoli (p.44)
Thursday	Tomato & Lentil soup (p.25)
Friday	Apple and Bean salad (p. 35) + veggie sausages
Saturday	Eat rest of salad + sausages
Sunday	Spanish Risotto (p. 52)

Check cupboards

pickles
tomato sauce
oil
lentils
garlic
stock cubes
marmite
lemon juice
mustard
chives
rice

Shopping

1 small bag potatoes
1 carrot
4 onions
3 mushrooms
1 small courgette
1 leek
1 yellow pepper
small piece broccoli
1 lettuce
tomatoes
half cucumber
spring onions
1 red dessert apple
fruit for snacks
1 bag plain crisps

dried fruit and nuts for snacks
bread
6 eggs
butter or spread
milk
large block cheese
4 vegetarian sausages
penne pasta
2 x 400g tin chopped tomatoes
1 x 400g tin bortolli beans
small pack pine nuts
1 jar green pesto
150g pack frozen broad beans

This shopping list assumes that you will eat sandwiches, fruit, or jacket potatoes for lunch each day. You will need to cook 5 times in the week.

Menu 4

Monday	Roast Tomatoes + Spaghetti (p.49)
Tuesday	French Onion Soup (p.24)
Wednesday	Cheesy Rice Slice + salad (p.55)
Thursday	Eat rest of Cheesy Rice Slice
Friday	Chick Pea + Feta Salad (p.32)
Saturday	Spaghetti Bolognese (p.40)
Sunday	Eat rest of Bolognese with jacket potato

Check cupboards

oil
spaghetti
chives
red lentils
stock cubes
marmite
salad dressing
curry paste

Shopping

1 small bag potatoes
1 carrot
1 celery
1 red pepper
1 small courgette
5 onions
1 bag spinach
small pack cherry tomatoes
fruit for snacks
1 lettuce
tomatoes
half cucumber
spring onions
1 small tub of cream

dried fruit and nuts for snacks
bread
butter or spread
milk
6 eggs
large block cheese
200g block feta cheese
small bottle black olives
1 x 400g tin chopped tomatoes
parmesan cheese
1 x 400g tin chick peas
1 small pot natural yogurt

This shopping list assumes that you will eat sandwiches, fruit, or jacket potatoes for lunch each day. You will need to cook 5 times in the week.

Index

I studied Textile Design at Loughborough College of Art and Design from 1990 – 1994. Since then I have worked as a freelance designer. I have been married to Ron for 26 years, and ours sons Ben and Tim have both graduated.

I started to cook cakes when I was 5 years old; by the time I was 12 my sister, Hilary, and I could cook a Sunday lunch! We would still have to do the washing up afterwards though! I have always loved cooking, especially for others, and there is nothing I like more than a house full of people to feed.

I am pleased with the feedback I have had from students regarding nosh4students and hope that this vegetarian edition proves to be equally helpful to vegetarian students. My aim is that you enjoy cooking and have a healthy diet.